IT HAPPENED ON
THE OUTER BANKS

D1304438

It Happened In Series

IT HAPPENED ON
THE OUTER BANKS

Molly Perkins Harrison

TWODOT®

GUILFORD, CONNECTICUT
HELENA, MONTANA
AN IMPRINT OF THE GLOBE PEQUOT PRESS

A · T W O D O T® · B O O K

Copyright © 2005 Morris Book Publishing, LLC

Map by Sue Cary © Morris Book Publishing, LLC

Library of Congress Cataloging-in-Publication Data
Harrison, Molly.
    It happened on the Outer Banks/Molly Harrison.—1st ed.
        p. cm.—(It happened in series)
    Includes bibliographical references.
    ISBN 978-0-7627-2707-0
        1. Outer Banks (N.C.)—History—Anecdotes. I. Title. II. Series.

F262.O96H37 2005
975.6'1—dc22

                                                                2005040349

Manufactured in the United States of America
First Edition/Third Printing

For Burch

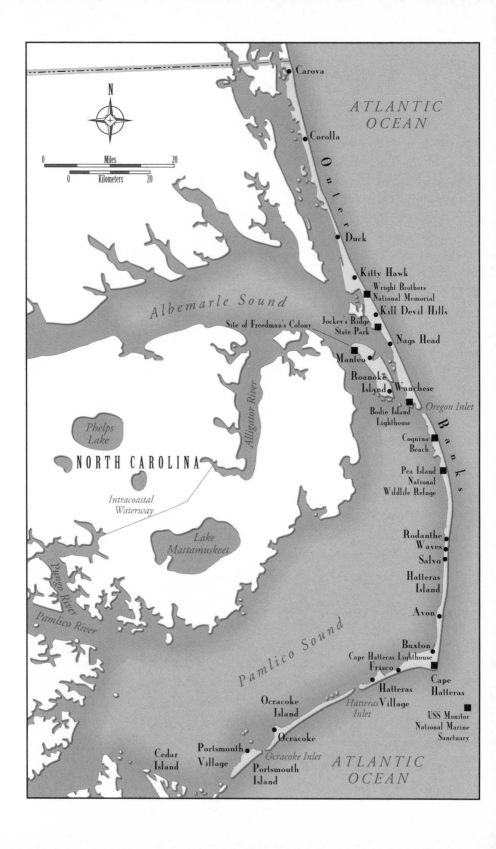

Contents

Preface

Seen on a map, the Outer Banks may not seem like much more than inconsequential strips of sand awash off the coast of North Carolina. Surrounded by the Atlantic Ocean and a vast system of brackish sounds, the slender barrier islands lie just offshore and stretch along the coast for over a hundred miles, but at most places they are barely a half-mile wide. From the map these islands may seem mere repositories for washed-up seashells or isolated sanctuaries for waterfowl and shorebirds.

But when you come here, you see that the Outer Banks is teeming with activity and life. In the last several decades hundreds of thousands of vacationers have discovered these islands, coming here mainly for outdoor recreational activities like surfing, swimming, fishing, and water sports. The Outer Banks offers a mix of preserved open spaces for wildlife and spectacular outdoor recreation to balance out all the usual vacation amenities, including accommodations, restaurants, shops, and attractions.

The Outer Banks, however, is far more than just a wild island landscape or a vacation destination. These islands have incredible stories to tell, dating back four centuries for English-speaking people, and well beyond that for Native Americans. And the Outer Banks' place in history is not just local or regional—important moments in our national history happened here.

Consider that the very first attempt to establish an English-speaking colony in North America occurred right here. Or that some of the important events of the early Civil War took place on the islands. You probably know that the Wright brothers learned to fly near Kitty Hawk, but did you know that the first musical notes ever to cross the airwaves were transmitted from Hatteras Island to Roanoke Island? Notable events in African-American history occurred here, including a colony for freed slaves on Roanoke Island starting in 1862, as well as the only all-black U.S. Life-Saving Service crew in the nation, which worked on Pea Island in the late nineteenth century. National military history was made on Hatteras Island in the 1920s when General Billy Mitchell proved that airplanes could sink battleships and again during World War II when German U-boats lurked off the coast and dealt a serious blow to Allied shipping. The Outer Banks is the home of the first national marine sanctuary as well as the first national seashore. The Carolina boat, a style of sport-fishing boat known the world over, was created here, and world-renowned sport fishing in the Gulf Stream off the coast of the Outer Banks is the stuff of legends.

The history of the Outer Banks is inextricably linked with the sea and the weather. Tales of storms and shipwrecks, lighthouses, and lifesaving permeate the culture here, and they factor into almost every story in this book. Because of the hardships of living so closely with the unpredictability of sea and weather, the people of the Outer Banks are hardy and strong, as you'll see in these stories.

In the following twenty-six stories, we hope you'll discover things you didn't know about the Outer Banks. We hope the stories will bring relevance to many things you see and experience on the modern-day Outer Banks. The stories span more than four hundred years, from early exploration in 1584 to a mass whale beaching in 2005. Of course there was no way to include all of the relevant historical events of the Outer Banks, but we think this selection gives a good overview of the Outer Banks' past and present.

Acknowledgments

Thanks to my editor, Stephanie Hester, for her patience and flexibility all throughout this project, but especially when my son was born a little bit earlier than expected. Thanks also to copyeditor Annie Beaver for her clarity and keen eye. I can't name them all here, but I am grateful to everyone I have interviewed over the years for this and other projects, all those people who have been willing to patiently and generously share their memories and knowledge with me. The staffs of the Outer Banks History Center and the Dare County Library, as always, were most helpful in providing research materials. Thanks to my husband and my family and friends for always listening and encouraging me and understanding when I couldn't come out to play because I was writing.

A Promising First Impression
· 1584 ·

The Englishmen watched in wonder as a small boat slowly made its way across the water, its occupants rowing it deftly in their direction. As the boat neared and the Englishmen could see the passengers, they knew to expect an encounter unlike any they had ever had before. Three dark-haired, dark-skinned, bare-chested men rowed the boat toward the two English ships, which the sailors had anchored inside an area they called "Port Ferdinando," near Roanoke Island. These were the first New World natives they had seen since they arrived on this stretch of coast just two days earlier, on July 13, 1584, and claimed the land for Queen Elizabeth.

One of the dark-haired men left the boat and boldly walked up to the point of land nearest the English ships. He paced the point until Captains Arthur Barlowe and Philip Amadas rowed in to greet him. The stranger was completely unafraid. Arthur Barlowe noted the following details of the meeting in his journal:

> And after he had spoken of many things not under-
> stood by us, we brought him with his own good lik-
> ing, aboard the ships, and gave him a shirt, and hat
> & some other things, and made him taste of our
> wine, and our meat, which he liked very well.

To show his gratitude, the native went back to his own boat and "fell to fishing," as Barlowe described. In less than half an hour, he and the others had filled the boat with fish. He divided the catch in half, leaving half of it on the point near the ships for the Englishmen. With that kind gesture, the natives departed, rowing across the sound until they were out of sight.

The next day several boats and as many as fifty natives greeted the Englishmen. Barlowe described the visitors as "very handsome, and goodly people, and in their behaviour as mannerly, and civill, as any in Europe." Leading this massive group was Granganimeo, brother of the region's king, Wingina. The Englishmen learned that the natives called the region Wingandacoa. The natives spread out a long mat upon the ground. Granganimeo and four others sat down and the rest of the men stood at a distance behind them. The Englishmen approached with their weapons, but the natives were unalarmed. Barlowe wrote:

> Sitting still [Granganimeo] beckoned us to come and sit by him, which we performed: and being set he made all signs of joy and welcome, striking on his head and his breast and afterwards on ours, to show we were all one, smiling and making show the best he could of all love, and familiarity. After he had made a long speech unto us, we presented him with divers [sic] things, which he received joyfully, and thankfully.

Through gestures and very few words, the Englishmen learned from Granganimeo that King Wingina had been wounded in a battle with the king of the next country, and this was the reason he had not come to greet them. The natives returned numerous times, and the two parties made many exchanges of goods. The natives wanted tin and copper pots and tools like axes, knives, and hatchets. Granganimeo was particularly taken with a tin dish, which he placed over his chest, motioning that it would protect him in battle. In exchange, the natives offered abundant "corrall" (shells), skins and hides, and food. Granganimeo and his men desperately wanted the Englishmen's armor, swords, and weapons, but as Barlowe said, "we would not depart with any." Granganimeo offered a great box of pearls in exchange for them, and every day he came with hares, fish, deer meat, melons, walnuts, cucumbers, gourds, peas, roots, and corn, hoping to change their minds. But the Englishmen wouldn't budge.

Later, Granganimeo brought his wife and daughter and little children to the ships to meet the Englishmen. Barlowe described Grangamineo's wife in his journal:

> . . . his wife was very well favored, of meane stature, and very bashfull: she had on her backe a long cloke of leather, with the furre side next to her bodie, and before her a peece of the same: about her forehead, she had a broad bande of white Corrall . . . in her eares she had bracelets of pearls, hanging down to her middle, and those were signes of good pease.

After the natives had been onboard the English ships numerous times, the Englishmen were invited to the natives' island home, which they called Roanoke. In their small rowing boats, the Englishmen followed the natives through the Croatan Sound to their village on the north end of the island. The village consisted of nine cedar houses, fortified by a circle of trees. Granganimeo's wife ran to greet the Englishmen. She ordered some of her people to pull their boats to shore and to bring their oars into the house so they wouldn't be stolen. The native woman invited them into her home to sit by the fire. She and the other women in the house washed their clothes and socks; a few of the Englishmen even had their feet washed.

Granganimeo's wife set everything, said Barlowe, in the "best manner shee coulde, making great haste to dresse some meate for us to eate." She fed them venison, roasted fish, melons, roots, fruits, and water steeped with herbs. Barlowe was obviously impressed:

> We were entertained with all love and kindness, and with as much bounty (after their manner) as they could possibly devise. We found the people most gentle, loving, and faithful, void of all guile and treason, and such as lived after the manner of the golden age.

As the Englishmen were eating, three native men came into the house with their bows and arrows, just returning from a hunting trip. The Englishmen eyed each other nervously and reached for their weapons. Seeing this, Granganimeo's wife ordered the native men to leave and to drop their bows and arrows.When it came time for the Englishmen to leave, the native woman urged them to sleep in the house. Though they trusted the natives, the Englishmen did not want to risk anything. "There was no cause of doubt: for a more kinde, and loving people, there can not be found in this world, as farre as we have hitherto had triall," wrote Barlowe. When they insisted on leaving, Granganimeo's wife loaded their boats with the rest of the dinner, bowls and all. The men rowed out away from shore and slept in their boats. When it rained that night, the native woman sent out someone with mats for the Englishmen to use as cover.

After this evening of friendship on Roanoke Island, the Englishmen went back to their ships the next day and left Roanoke Island to further explore the area. They explored the mainland and the nearby barrier islands, encountering other natives and learning of the various area tribes and kings and lands. The Englishmen returned to Roanoke Island in August, just before heading back to England. Traveling with them were two "Savages" (as the Englishmen called the natives) from Roanoke Island, men by the names of Manteo and Wanchese, to introduce to Sir Walter Raleigh, who was paying for this exploration of the New World and wanted to know everything about it.

The description of Roanoke Island that Amadas and Barlowe took back to Queen Elizabeth and Sir Walter Raleigh in England was promising. Their first impression was quite favorable, for they had seen Roanoke Island and the surrounding barrier islands in midsummer, when the islands were in full bloom and the natives were generous because, at the time, food was plentiful. Queen Elizabeth, pleased with Amadas and Barlowe's report of friendly natives and lush islands, claimed the land, named it Virginia, and put Sir Walter Raleigh in charge as chief lord of the new territory.

Later, when Sir Walter Raleigh sent over more Englishmen to attempt colonization on Roanoke Island, they would see the flip side of that rosy picture. In winter, when supplies on the barrier islands were scarce, both the Englishmen and the natives, so friendly to each other at first, would see each other in a new light. They would learn firsthand the difficulties and hardships of two diverse cultures sharing a small island.

Blackbeard Goes Down

·1718·

From his position on the ocean side of Ocracoke Inlet, Lieutenant Robert Maynard saw a mast rising up behind the dunes across the island. Captain Edward Teach, the notorious pirate called Blackbeard, the man whose head he hunted, was right where Maynard had heard he would be—tucked into a protected sound-side bay on the southern tip of Ocracoke Island.

Maynard was unfamiliar with Ocracoke Inlet and night was falling, so he decided to wait until daylight to cross over to the Pamlico Sound and attack the pirate's ship. He ordered the crew to anchor the two sloops he had sailed down from Virginia and kept a vigilant eye on the inlet. Teach didn't even appear to have a sentinel ship watching his back. Was capturing the despicable pirate going to be as easy as it seemed?

Maynard had been sent on this mission to find and kill Edward Teach by Governor Alexander Spotswood of Virginia. Teach, commonly known as Blackbeard for the thick dark beard that obscured the lower half of his face, had been terrorizing the mid-Atlantic coast for only a year, but his escapades had been audacious and destructive, and he was a formidable threat in the eyes of merchantmen and seamen all along the East Coast. He had learned the tricks of the trade in 1716 from the fiercest of all pirates, Captain Benjamin

Hornigold, in the West Indies. Then in the winter of 1717–1718, Blackbeard captained of his own fleet of ships, the *Queen Anne's Revenge,* the *Revenge,* and the *Adventure,* and terrorized the coasts of Delaware, Virginia, the Carolinas and Florida. It was a profligate binge of piracy, capturing ships of all nationalities and pillaging them of all their goods. In addition, for several days in May of 1718, he blockaded the entire port city of Charles Towne, South Carolina, the southern colonies' busiest port, holding civilians hostage and demanding medicine for his crew. In June 1718, Teach decided to settle down in Bath Town, North Carolina, and live a law-abiding life with a sixteen-year-old bride, who was reputed to be his fourteenth wife. However, he soon grew bored with the gentleman's life and took back to the seas. It wasn't long before tales of his piracy again spread among the British colonies.

In the fall of 1718, Governor Spotswood's men captured Blackbeard's quartermaster, William Howard, and learned of the pirate's Ocracoke Island hideout. Howard also confessed that Blackbeard had only one ship at the time, the *Adventure,* and a small crew of about eighteen men working with him onboard the sloop. Spotswood, who was sinking down in favor with his own governing council and the people of the Virginia colony, used this information to his advantage. If he could catch this well-known criminal, he thought, it would certainly restore his worthiness in the eyes of the people of Virginia. Plus, he imagined, there might be some material gain, as Teach was believed to hold great treasure.

The mission to track down Blackbeard was a secret. Without consulting Virginia's governing council and at his own expense, Spotswood sent Lieutenant Maynard of the British Royal Navy out of Hampton, Virginia, with two armed sloops, the *Jane* and the *Ranger,* along with fifty-three men trained for battle. They arrived at Ocracoke Island on November 21, 1718.

Early in the morning of November 22, Maynard roused his crew and raised the anchors. He sent forth a rowboat to navigate the deepest course through the inlet so his ships could follow. But it didn't take long for the men on the *Adventure* to spy the rowboat and the two formidable sloops behind it. Blackbeard's crew fired guns at the rowboat, which hastily retreated back to the Navy sloops. Maynard raised the Union Jack, the flag signaling the ships' affiliation with the British Navy.

Instead of retreating back through the Pamlico Sound, as he could have very easily done, Blackbeard sailed the *Adventure* straight for the Navy ships. Masterfully navigating the waters he knew so well, Blackbeard then sailed toward the beach, slipping into a narrow slough between a sandbar and the shore. The *Jane* and the *Ranger* followed, but not closely enough, and soon they were grounded on the sandbar, tricked by the pirate and unable to move.

Blackbeard and Maynard shouted at each other across the water, each promising doom to the other. As Maynard's crew struggled to free their ships from the sandbar by throwing over the ballast and water barrels, Blackbeard's men fired eight cannon to the broadside of the immobile Navy ships. The *Ranger* was badly damaged, and nearly twenty men were either killed or wounded. However, the force of the cannon firing also forced Blackbeard's *Adventure* aground as well. Soon, though, the wind picked up and all three ships were blown free of the sandbar and into the sea.

Blackbeard struck again, this time with grenades his crew had made by filling glass bottles with gunpowder, shot, lead, and fuses. They hurled the grenades at the *Jane,* and the air rocked with explosions and great clouds of smoke.

In the midst of the smoke and fire, Maynard ordered his remaining crew into the hold with their weapons ready. He left the bodies of his wounded and dead men on the decks and retreated down below with his men. As the smoke cleared, Blackbeard saw only the men lying on the decks, some stirring in agony but most still. Thinking he had killed the majority of his attackers, the pirate sailed the *Adventure* right up alongside the *Jane,* lashed his boat taught to it, and brazenly boarded the enemy ship.

As Blackbeard victoriously tramped across the bloody deck, surveying the dead bodies, Maynard's crew spilled from the hold, racing toward the pirate and his crew. The Royal Navy seamen fought with the rugged pirates, swords clanging, pistols firing, shouts piercing the air.

Maynard fought his way toward Blackbeard. Both of the men pulled out a pistol and fired at the other. Blackbeard's shot missed, but Maynard's bullet struck the pirate, who kept on fighting despite the gunshot wound. The men then began to battle with swords, and Blackbeard's swipe was so hard it broke Maynard's sword in two. Just as Blackbeard was closing in to kill Maynard, one of the British seamen stabbed the pirate from behind, slicing him in the neck and throat. With blood gushing from his neck, Blackbeard continued to fight, swinging his sword wildly. When they could get to him, British seamen stabbed him repeatedly in the back. Blackbeard raised his pistol and was about to fire it one last time when he finally died, collapsing onto the deck.

It had taken five gunshot wounds and twenty severe stabs to take down the legendary pirate. Maynard ordered Blackbeard's head severed from his body. He threw his body overboard and tied his head to his bowsprit for the sail back to Virginia.

Blackbeard's Ocracoke Island hideout is still remembered today. The cove on the southern tip of the island where he used to lay low and congregate with other pirates is still known as Teach's Hole.

Lighting the Graveyard of the Atlantic

·1772·

The *Thunderbolt,* making her way from the Caribbean island of St. Croix to New York City by wind power alone, listed hard to one side. The passengers, in their berths and on the decks, gripped the nearest supports they could find, a wave of fear buckling their knees for the first time since they'd started this sailing journey up the Atlantic coast.

The sloop's crew made preparations to round Cape Hatteras, the sharp point at the center of the North Carolina coast, always the most tumultuous patch of sea along this route. Passengers were ushered below deck, and supplies were secured. Captain William Newton was vigilant, determined to ensure that his vessel cut its way through the messy convergence of sea currents without washing toward the cape's dreaded shoals. Fear jolted through his veins as well, but to keep the crew and the passengers calm, he did his best not to let it show. The weather conditions were not ideal for sailing on this part of the coast: The winds were rising just as the *Thunderbolt* approached the infamous cape.

As the winds increased and the ship rocked on the stormy seas, young Alexander Hamilton, on his first ocean voyage, was on edge. Up to this point the trip had been smooth sailing along the Gulf Stream, but now the seas were violent, harsh. The water was dark, gray, and menacing, not at all like the clear, calm, aqua blue he was used to at home in the islands. Waves of nausea washed over him as the seas washed over the decks. Books, clothes, and belongings spilled all over his berth and rattled back and forth as the ship tossed on the seas.

Hamilton tried to remain calm, to hold tightly in one place, but when his nose caught a whiff of smoke, he became alarmed. Peeking out of his berth, he saw a plume of smoke rising from the ship and heard a crewman ordering everyone onto the decks. The passengers moved with trepidation, clutching walls and rails to keep their balance.

Then people began shouting. The ship was on fire! The wild rocking of the boat had caused hot coals to spill from the cooking fire and ignite the wooden ship. Chaos ensued, with the crew slinging buckets of salt water onto the fire. The passengers watched in horror as the fire caught the corner of a sail. With astonishing speed, the flames climbed up the cloth.

The crew snapped their attention to the flaming sails, dowsing them with sprays of water. Soon the fire was quelled but the sails were badly damaged and the ship severely disabled. With no way to catch the wind, the captain struggled to guide the ship eastward, away from the Outer Banks. He knew there wasn't much hope for an out-of-control ship at Cape Hatteras. Once grounded on the shoals of the cape, a ship's certain fate was a slow pounding to bits by the torrential seas.

For Hamilton, who was only seventeen years old, the early days of the trip had allowed him time to dream of his new life in the North American colonies and the formal education that awaited him there. The fact that he might never even make it onto the land of his dreams was hard to think about. It seemed to him a matter of luck that he was on the ship at all, and it also seemed that his luck was drying up.

A particularly destructive hurricane that struck St. Croix on August 31, 1772, had inspired Hamilton to write an impassioned letter to his father, who lived on another Caribbean island, about the plight of the people in St. Croix. A local minister somehow came upon the letter and, because it was so well-written, had it published in the island's newspaper. The letter was so poetic and thoughtful that the minister and several wealthy residents of St. Croix established a fund to educate its surprisingly intelligent writer. At the behest of these benefactors, Hamilton set sail on the *Thunderbolt* several months later, bound for New York. The dream he'd had of attending a college in North America was finally coming true.

But standing on the deck of the partially burned, sail-less ship being tossed about the ocean waves like a toy, Hamilton doubted he would ever see New York or the inside of a university. He doubted he would ever see anything beyond this ghastly, terrifying stretch of sea.

Fate proved otherwise. Captain Newton was an experienced sailor, and his seafaring prowess prevailed. He managed to steer the broken ship around the stormy seas at Cape Hatteras, a task most ship's captains would have failed. Though the trip was arduous, the *Thunderbolt* eventually reached its destination. Hamilton would go to college after all.

Seventeen years later, after attending King's College (now Columbia University) in New York, Hamilton had made his mark as an American statesman. At the age of thirty-four, he was the second-ranking member of George Washington's cabinet, in charge of the new nation's Treasury Department.

In his position in Washington, Hamilton heard complaints of the treacherous waters off the coast of Cape Hatteras, of which he had firsthand knowledge. He heard of the horrors of sailors who had barely escaped with their lives and of those who weren't so lucky. Sailors and frequent sea travelers pleaded with the government to build a lighthouse to help in navigating this dangerous stretch of coast.

Cape Hatteras was an unavoidable point on the vital trade routes between the United States, Europe, and the Caribbean. Just off Cape Hatteras, the Atlantic's fastest-flowing currents met. These currents are the south-flowing Labrador Current and the north-flowing Gulf Stream, and they were extremely useful to sailors because ships could hitch a ride on the current flowing in either direction and shave days off the length of their trips. But the currents did not offer a totally free ride. A ride on either current brought ships right past the shoals of Cape Hatteras. In addition, the two currents intersected at the cape, creating turbulent waters and constantly shifting shoals. Captains had to be careful to steer east of the cape's dangerous, unpredictable shoals, and they needed a lighthouse to help them do so.

Hamilton remembered his own near-tragic experience off Cape Hatteras. He had not forgotten the terror of being tossed uncontrollably on the stormy seas, wondering whether or not he would survive to tell the tale. He began to refer to the area around Cape Hatteras as "The Graveyard of the Atlantic," a name that has stuck for more than 200 years.

In 1789 Hamilton urged the United States Congress to construct a lighthouse at Cape Hatteras. Congress thus enacted the Lighthouse Bill, which started the process of establishing a network of lighthouses on the East Coast, making sea travel safer and more efficient. The bill required that lighthouses already under construction or already built be deeded over to the United States, and for all maintenance and repair of lighthouses to fall under the jurisdiction of the U.S. Treasury Department.

Hamilton sent Commissioner of Revenue Tenche Cox to Hatteras Island to find a piece of land on which to construct the Cape Hatteras Lighthouse. Cox selected four acres of dunes owned by the Jennett family and paid them $50 for the property.

The Cape Hatteras Lighthouse was authorized by Congress in 1794, but it would take another eight years to complete North Carolina's third but most important beacon.

In November 1798, Henry Dearborn received $8,000 to purchase materials for the Cape Hatteras Lighthouse. However, because of difficulties in shipping the lighthouse materials, construction was delayed until September 1799. Bringing the materials to Hatteras Island presented obstacles no one had predicted. The heavily laden cargo ships that came in across the Pamlico Sound could not reach the western shore of the island because the water was too shallow. All of the cargo had to be transferred to flat-bottom craft, called lighters, to be transported to land. Once ashore, transporting the materials across the soft, sandy island was equally as difficult. Wooden tracks had to be laid across the island and oxen used to pull the stone, granite, iron, and other materials across the tracks to the east side of the island. To top it off, the mosquitoes and flies were horrendous.

To start the project, Dearborn had a 13-foot-deep hole dug to build a solid stone foundation underground. The foundation was poured from a mortar made by burning oyster shells at the site. The foundation was topped by a granite base 9 feet thick and 9 feet high. At this point, winter weather delayed work until the spring of 1800. But Dearborn had to leave to tend to other projects, and the workers were plagued with sickness. A few even died. It was the spring of 1801 before Dearborn returned his attention to the project. The octagonal tower, at a height of 90 feet, was finally completed in 1802.

The tower was capped by a 10-foot-high glass-enclosed lantern room and covered by a 5-foot-high roof. A wooden stairway wound through the interior to the lantern chamber, where the lamps were fueled by whale oil. Adam Gaskins was selected as the first keeper, and the Cape Hatteras Lighthouse was fully operational in early 1803. With the lamps a hundred feet above ground, the light could be seen 12 miles out to sea in clear weather.

Unfortunately, sailors and sea captains were immediately disappointed with the Cape Hatteras Lighthouse. Since the weather was rarely clear at the cape and the shoals extended more than 12 miles from shore, the light was essentially worthless. Captain David D. Porter wrote to the Lighthouse Board, saying, "I know nothing of the lights on Capes Henlopen, May, and Henry, and will proceed to speak of Hatteras Light, the most important on our coast, and, without doubt, the *worst* light in the world."

The first Cape Hatteras Lighthouse was improved upon as much as possible over the years, until a second, more useful, lighthouse was finally built nearly seven decades later. Alexander Hamilton's vision of protecting sailors in "The Graveyard of the Atlantic" was realized in 1870 with the lighting of the second Cape Hatteras Lighthouse, which still guards the infamous Cape Hatteras shoals today.

The Storm That Sliced the Islands

· 1846 ·

After days of relentless northeast winds, the waters were shoved out of the Pamlico Sound, exposing jagged oyster and mussel beds on the muddy bottom. The Atlantic Ocean was fierce from the gale, its waves swallowing the beaches of the Outer Banks.

But on the morning of September 7, 1846, the steady northeast winds finally died out, leaving behind a clear and calm day. C. O. Boutelle, the assistant superintendent of the U.S. Coast Guard Survey, was working out in the field on Bodie Island. An acquaintance of his, a Mr. Midgett, was on horseback, conducting some sort of business in the same area. Many people must have come out of their homes to see the sun that morning, after having hunkered down indoors during the nor'easter. Little did the Banks residents know that a hurricane was stalking the North Carolina coast, hovering just offshore, waiting for just the right time to strike.

The calm that had settled over the area disappeared at about 11:00 A.M. As the eye of the storm made its pass over the Outer Banks, the winds snapped violently around to the southwest. A massive volume of water surged back into the Pamlico Sound and washed entirely across Bodie and Hatteras Islands to meet with the sea. "The sound waters overflowed the whole island, leaving only the tops of the highest sand knolls bare," Boutelle later said, estimating that the mean flood level was 5½ feet above the sand flat. In one place, he said, the water broke over the top of a 7-foot post.

Midgett and his horse fled to a sandy knoll, where they waited five hours for the floodwaters to subside. Midgett was less than a mile from home, but he was helpless, trapped on all sides by swirling waters, wondering if the waves were going to sweep him away, but worrying more about what was happening to his family and his property farther down on Bodie Island. Destruction was rampant all along the southern Outer Banks. Houses, boats, and livestock floated out to sea. Great, sprawling live oaks were uprooted and tumbled away on the waves. Residents in Hatteras were appalled to see the sound meeting the sea in the places where their houses had once stood and their gardens had once grown.

In the aftermath of the storm, as the waters began to recede, it was clear that some of the sound-to-sea meeting places were there to stay. Redding R. Quidley, who worked as a pilot at Ocracoke Inlet, discovered that a new cut had sliced through his home turf. His land—where he and his brother had cut yaupon and his uncle had grown figs and peaches—was underwater. Soon, the cut grew into a large inlet, forming two islands, Hatteras and Ocracoke, and preventing him from walking to work at Ocracoke as he was used to doing. He later said:

> There was nothing to cause me or anyone, to have any idea that there would be an inlet there, sooner than any other part of the beach; there was no water passed over the place except in those heavy easterly gales, when as a general thing it passes over nearly all our beach from Hatteras to Ocracoke. The day the inlet was cut out, there were several families living where the inlet is now.

This inlet came to be known as Hatteras Inlet, named after the land it cut across and after another inlet of the same name that had filled in completely in 1764.

To the north, at Bodie Island, the storm had formed two new inlets. The sound-to-sea sluices were insignificant at first, with the northern one being the deepest and widest. Throughout the month of September, westerly winds prevailed and the sound waters gradually cut the inlets wider. The northern inlet eventually filled in with sediment, but the southern one expanded exponentially. Boutelle reported that the southern inlet eventually came to measure 202 yards wide at high tide and 107 yards at low tide. This inlet later came to be known as Oregon Inlet, named after the first ship that passed through it, the *Oregon*.

The new inlets changed not only the geography of the Outer Banks, but also the way of life. Prior to the opening of Hatteras and Oregon inlets, Ocracoke Inlet was the only navigable inlet through the Banks between Beaufort and Virginia. Though Ocracoke Inlet was prone to develop shoals and often difficult to navigate, it was the primary point of entry for mercantile vessels headed to or from the populous areas of northeastern North Carolina. Maritime traffic through Ocracoke Inlet was brisk. During the late eighteenth and early nineteenth centuries, up to thirty or forty vessels at a time would wait inside the inlet to pass out to sea. On either side of the inlet, the villages of Portsmouth and Ocracoke prospered, with taverns, shops, hotels, and even a hospital. The census in 1840 listed 531 residents at Ocracoke and 400 at Portsmouth.

But the opening of Hatteras Inlet changed all that. The new inlet marked the beginning of the end for Portsmouth Village. As Hatteras Inlet widened and deepened, pilots eyeballed it as an alternative to the notoriously difficult-to-navigate Ocracoke Inlet. On February 5, 1847, just five months after the storm, Redding Quidley, who had always piloted ships through Ocracoke Inlet, guided the first vessel—the inward-bound schooner *Asher C. Havens*—through Hatteras Inlet. Quidley also piloted the first outbound vessel, a small steamer.

During the Civil War, maritime traffic ceased through the Union-controlled inlet, but after the war, Hatteras replaced Ocracoke as the main inlet of entry through the southern Outer Banks. Portsmouth had lost its industry. Attempts were made to start oil and menhaden fishery industries there, but none succeeded. With the decline of maritime traffic through the inlet also came a population decline as the villagers left the island to find work. In 1850 there had been 505 residents, but by 1950 there were only 14. Today there are no permanent residents on Portsmouth Island. Ocracoke Inlet still exists and is used by commercial and recreational boaters on Ocracoke Island.

Today, both Hatteras and Oregon inlets are navigable and highly depended upon in commercial and recreational fishing. It's rare for storm-induced inlets to last for more than 150 years; left in their natural state, most inlets migrate south and close after a short while. In the case of these two inlets, they have become such integral parts of Outer Banks life that man has fought their natural migration and closure with constant dredging.

Hatteras Inlet is a risky but dependable traverse, used by commercial and recreational fishermen to head out to the Gulf Stream. An hourly stream of ferries crosses Hatteras Inlet every day, transporting people and cars over land that was once filled with yaupon, sprawling live oaks, and "a fine potato patch," according to Redding R. Quidley, who used to walk through there on his way to work.

Oregon Inlet today is treacherous and unstable, naturally trying to close while man tries desperately to keep it open. Since 1846, the littoral current has moved the inlet markedly to the south. The south shore has been cut away while the north shore has built up with sand. But because it's used extensively by both recreational and commercial fishermen (yet is regarded as one of the most dangerous inlets on the East Coast), Oregon

Inlet is constantly dredged and maintained. For a decade there was much debate about building jetties to stabilize the inlet, with environmentalists and geologists highly opposed to the idea and the fishermen who depend on the inlet strongly in favor. The jetty project is not going to happen anytime soon, as was finally declared in 2003 after a decade of debate, but the inlet will continue to be dredged to keep it open. Its closure would significantly alter an established way of life.

As many as twenty inlets have opened and closed along the Outer Banks in the past four centuries, but the only other permanent inlets since the storm of September 1846 have occurred in the unpopulated Core Banks, south of Ocracoke. The two inlets that have developed most recently occurred just north of Buxton in 1962 and just north of Hatteras Village in 2003, but both of these were immediately filled with sand by the state of North Carolina because their presence was just too disrupting for the residents of Hatteras Island.

The possibility always exists that another major hurricane will hit the Outer Banks, creating new cuts through the fences of barrier islands that separate the sounds from the sea. Each inlet's opening and closing is proof that change is constant on the Outer Banks and no one ever knows what the next storm will bring.

The Chicamacomico Races

• 1861 •

Nothing, not even the balmy southwest winds on Hatteras Island, could ease Col. Rush Hawkins's mind. Since taking over the Confederate forts Hatteras and Clark less than a month ago, the Union colonel was restless with wonder over how the Confederates planned to get their forts back in their control.

Hawkins had more than 1,500 men under his command. Nine hundred of them were from the Ninth and Twentieth New York Volunteers, 600 were from the Twentieth Indiana, plus a company of First U.S. Artillery, and all of them camped in and around the two hastily built forts on the lonely sand banks of Hatteras Inlet. In addition, he had five small, armed naval vessels. But none of these forces made him feel comfortable or secure. He was convinced that the Confederates, who had fled 50 miles away to Roanoke Island when their forts were captured, were assembling larger forces and planning an attack to recapture Forts Hatteras and Clark.

Hawkins knew the importance of safeguarding the two forts that guarded Hatteras Inlet, which was easily the deepest, most easily navigable passageway on the central North Carolina coast. Control of this inlet was vital to blocking Confederate supply runs to the port towns on the North Carolina mainland, and Hawkins intended to keep these forts in Union control, choking off the Confederate supply lines.

In late September 1861, he decided he could not wait and wonder anymore. Hawkins ordered Col. W. L. Brown to move the 600 men of the Twentieth Indiana 30 miles north to the Hatteras Island village of Chicamacomico. There, he believed, his men would be able to see Confederate ships when they moved from Roanoke Island toward Hatteras Inlet, as he fully expected they would, and be able to give him early warning of the anticipated Confederate attack. He sent the Indiana regiment marching off into the autumn heat with promises that the tug *Fanny* was right behind them, loaded with all the supplies they would need. Most important of these supplies was drinking water, a necessity in the desertlike conditions of the Outer Banks.

Meanwhile, on Roanoke Island, Confederate Col. A. E. Wright was just as ill at ease because he imagined that the Federals, who were much stronger in terms of men and supplies, were planning an attack on Roanoke Island. He, too, lived in constant anticipation of what the enemy might do next. And his troops—the Third Georgia and the Eighth North Carolina—and fleet of five shallow-draft steamers known as the "Mosquito Fleet" were not enough to instill a great sense of confidence in his abilities to stave off a Union attack.

On October 2, 1861, reports of the Union tug *Fanny* prowling northward up the Pamlico Sound played upon Wright's fears of an attack. He ordered the commander of the Mosquito Fleet, Commodore W. F. Lynch, "at once to intercept and capture her, and if possible to learn the intention of the enemy, who were evidently meditating some hostile movement upon his position." Three vessels of the Mosquito Fleet chased down the Fanny and went at her with guns firing. After only about a half-hour of fighting, the captain and much of the crew of the *Fanny* abandoned ship when a Confederate gun shell hit the deck. They hopped into their small boat, leaving dozens of Union soldiers onboard and easily giving the Confederates their first capture of a Union warship during the Civil War.

The Confederates seized the cargo onboard the *Fanny* and took the prisoners back to Roanoke Island. Upon questioning the prisoners, Wright learned of the 600 Union forces of the Indiana regiment at Chicamacomico. The Confederates valued the supplies and equipment taken from the *Fanny* at $150,000 and discovered a weak spot in the Union forces: They had intercepted their vital supply of drinking water.

Colonel Wright and Commodore Lynch formed a defensive plan of attack on the enemy. The Confederate forces would be shipped across the sound on all available vessels. The Third Georgia Infantry would land on Hatteras Island north of Chicamacomico, while the Eighth North Carolina would land to the south, forming a trap around the enemy camp. They would eliminate the Union forces at Chicamacomico, then march south to put out the light in the Cape Hatteras Lighthouse. From there they would march to Hatteras Inlet and recapture their forts.

Nothing ever goes as smoothly as planned.

In the pre-dawn hours of October 5, 1861, the Confederate forces steamed down Pamlico Sound toward Chicamacomico. Just as the sun was beginning to rise, they realized they had sailed a little closer to their enemy target than had been planned: They were within full view of the Union forces.

On the shore, Union commander Colonel Brown hastily sent a message requesting reinforcements to Colonel Hawkins at Hatteras Inlet. Brown lined up his forces in battle formation, and they all watched as the ships carrying the Third Georgia grounded on the shoals north of their camp. The Confederate soldiers struggled over the sides of the ships with their guns and equipment and laboriously waded through more than a mile of shallow water to the shore. The Union soldiers watched the other half of the Confederate ships steam south of the camp in an obvious attempt to trap them.

Instead of preparing for attack, Brown ordered his forces to retreat. His orders were for the Federals to march all the way back to the forts at Hatteras Inlet, more than 30 miles south. The 600 men of the Twentieth Indiana fled in panic, with no semblance of a military formation. They abandoned their camp and made haste down the banks. The men of the Third Georgia, who had finally made it to shore, followed close at their heels, firing guns as they ran. But most of the Georgia men stopped to raid the Federals' camp, which gave the Indiana soldiers a significant lead. The Georgia men were no doubt thinking that their comrades, the men of the Eighth North Carolina, would soon land farther down on Hatteras Island and close in on the retreating enemy from the south.

It was a scalding hot day, and the Union soldiers' retreat soon turned into a weary slog through the sand. Though they were surrounded by water on both sides of the island, they had none to drink. Many of the soldiers discarded their wool uniforms and trudged along half-naked throughout the morning and the afternoon. An Indiana soldier later wrote this of the scene:

> The sun was shining on the white sand of the beach, heating the air as if it were a furnace. The first ten miles was terrible. No water, the men unused to long marches, the sand heavy, their feet sinking into it at every step. As the regiment moved along, man after man would stagger from the ranks and fall upon the hot sand. . . . In every clump of bushes I would find men utterly exhausted. The enemy's vessels were now nearly opposite, steaming down the sound to cut off our retreat. I would tell them this, but they would say they did not care, they would die there, so utterly hopeless they did seem.

When the Indiana soldiers saw the Confederate ships approaching along the sound, they moved over to the ocean side of the island, out of the Confederates' sight. Thus, they weren't aware that the Confederate ships and soldiers were never able to make a landing on the island. Every time the ships attempted a landing, they ran aground, and every time the soldiers attempted to walk to shore, they encountered deep-water sloughs between the ships and the island and had to return to the ships.

The Georgia regiment was also unaware of this development. Fully expecting reinforcements at any minute, they pursued the Union soldiers all day long and into the night. Along the way they took about forty Union prisoners.

The bulk of the Union soldiers made it to the Cape Hatteras Lighthouse by midnight, finally finding water after their 23-mile trek. The Georgia soldiers camped about 9 miles north of the lighthouse, still unaware that their Confederate comrades had not closed in on the Union soldiers from the south.

At dawn the Georgia soldiers resumed their march in pursuit of their enemy. Upon approaching the lighthouse, Colonel Wright learned that the North Carolina regiment had never made landfall and he had no backup support. He ordered a complete about-face, turning his troops around to retreat 23 miles up the island to Chicamacomico.

Having sent a request for backup to the troops at Fort Hatteras, the Indiana soldiers now had backup troops, the Ninth New York, and they all began to chase the retreating Confederates back toward Chicamacomico. The Federal steamer *Monticello,* dispatched from Fort Hatteras after receiving the plea for help from Colonel Brown, fired upon the retreating Confederate soldiers from the water. The Union soldiers fired for hours, but they did little damage to the marching Confederate troops, who only suffered a few wounded soldiers. Their worries were much more focused on blistered feet, the heat, and trudging through the sand. A Georgia soldier later wrote the following:

> It was severe, I assure you. We marched upon the
> Sound side of the beach and of course a great part of

the way, across the little inlets, through water 2 and 3 feet deep. I marched till mired down, then I took off my pants, shoes and socks—which made me much lighter. Most of us did this, and most of us walk with difficulty yet because of sore feet. Those that took it barefooted stood the march the best. It was said to be the *Monticello* that attacked us. Of course we could offer no resistance, for they kept 3 or 4 large-sized guns belching forth death and destruction at us without any compunctions and we had to march down the beach and take it.

The Georgians reached Chicamacomico and the Mosquito Fleet well ahead of their on-land enemy pursuers. They boarded their ships and went back to Roanoke Island. The Union soldiers arrived back at the Chicamacomico camp but didn't stay long. Soon they marched back down the island to Forts Hatteras and Clark.

Both sides ended up where they started and nothing had been accomplished. All they had done was march up and down the Hatteras Sand Banks in the hot sun, in what would later be termed the "Chicamacomico Races."

Burnside Takes Roanoke Island

• 1862 •

I fear for Roanoke Island.
—Confederate Brig. Gen. D. H. Hill, October 1861

With a motley fleet of nearly eighty vessels, including barges, ships, transports, steamers, and tugs, as well as 13,000 Union troops, Brigadier General Ambrose E. Burnside's Coastal Division set sail from Fort Monroe in Hampton, Virginia, in January of 1862. Though some of Burnside's vessels had been deemed less than seaworthy, the leader instilled confidence in his troops by choosing to cruise on the smallest ship, *The Picket*.

It was the largest amphibious force to date, and their destination was a secret. Reporters knew the ships must be gathered for some strategic purpose, but no one who knew was giving any hints. Even President Lincoln was queried by journalists, but in typical Lincoln fashion, he had a wry answer for the reporters scrambling to cover the story. "Now I will tell you in great confidence where they are going, if you promise not to speak of it to anyone . . . the expedition is going to sea," President Lincoln quipped.

Burnside and the fleet were headed for North Carolina's Outer Banks, on a mission to gain control of Roanoke Island, which they saw as an important stepping-stone in their overall scheme to take over North Carolina's crucial port towns, thus cutting off Confederate supply lines. Burnside would get there via Hatteras Inlet, of which the Union had recently gained control. But getting to Roanoke Island would not be an easy breeze through the inlet.

As soon as the fleet reached Cape Hatteras, the area dubbed the Graveyard of the Atlantic began living up to its notorious reputation. The ships found Hatteras Inlet impassable due to the roiling waves and fierce wind. Burnside's mission, caught in a winter storm, was off to a treacherous start.

The ships waited for days for the gale to subside and the inlet waters to settle down. Burnside's vessels became clustered on the outer sandbar outside Hatteras Inlet without any formal formation or order, rollicking like toys in the choppy waves. Passenger vessels anchored to the outer bar smacked into one another in the chaos of the weather. "As far as the eye can reach, the water is rolling, foaming and dashing over the shoals, throwing its spray into the air," wrote Private D. L. Day on January 13.

The largest vessel of the fleet, an Army transport known as the *City of New York,* became grounded on the sandbar and sank, along with its cargo of supplies and ordnance. Its crew, clinging to the ship's rigging, was rescued in the knick of time. Another of Burnside's ships, the Army gunboat the *Zouave,* sank as well. One of Burnside's steamers, the *Pocahontas,* washed ashore, losing nearly 100 horses.

After days of rough weather, most of the other ships made it through the inlet by January 19, although some had to be towed by other vessels. Over the course of the next week, the remaining vessels straggled through the inlet. The exhausted, hungry, and thirsty Union troops rested on Hatteras Island, gathering strength for the battle to come at Roanoke Island. While on Hatteras, Burnside's luck turned around. He found valuable allies in former slaves from Roanoke Island who gave him useful information about Roanoke Island's geography, its waterways, and the Confederate military forts established there.

Even before the Union fleet arrived at Hatteras Inlet, the Confederates in North Carolina knew an attack on Roanoke Island was imminent. With the Outer Banks inlets and forts in Union hands, Roanoke Island was the next obvious target in the Union's plan to control the sounds, rivers, and ports of North Carolina. By January of 1862, Roanoke Island was outfitted with 1,400 Confederate troops and several small forts and ready for an attack. Three forts—Huger, Blanchard, and Bartow—were on the north end of the island and armed with twenty-five cannons. There was an unnamed fort on the east side of the island and a small stronghold in the center of the island, but the south end was left unguarded. The Confederates were counting on the dense marsh and swamp of the southern end of the island to protect them from a southerly invasion. The Confederate navy had dedicated seven small wooden boats, known as the "Mosquito Fleet," to the defense of Roanoke as well.

The island's military leader, Gen. Henry Wise, knew he was ill-prepared for an attack and begged Confederate leaders in Richmond for more troops, tools, ordnance, and supplies. His men were, in his own words, "undrilled, unpaid, not sufficiently clothed and quartered, and miserably armed with old flint muskets in bad order." But by the time his Mosquito Fleet's scouts reported the arrival of Burnside's troops at Hatteras Inlet, no help or supplies had arrived. The troops on Roanoke Island waited for the inevitable attack. Meanwhile, Wise became ill and was forced to retreat to a Nags Head hotel with a "violent and acute attack of pleurisy, with high fever and spitting of blood, threatening pneumonia." Command of Roanoke Island was transferred to Col. H. M. Shaw.

The Union armada sailed from Hatteras Inlet on February 5 to the tip of Stumpy Point, south of Roanoke Island. The next day they embarked toward the island but then had to stop and anchor in the sound because of fog and rain.

Finally, on February 7 at 10:30 A.M., the battle began at long range between the Confederate forts and the Union ships. Three

Union ships were hit; two withdrew and one sank. The firing continued until sunset, when both parties ceased for the day.

During the night, 200 Confederates on Roanoke Island peered out of the woods on the southwest end of the island. From their hiding place, they watched the Union ships unloading troops on Roanoke's sandy beach at Ashby's Harbor (called Skyco today). A steamer towing small boats would head toward the shoreline at full steam and then veer quickly away from shore and cast the lines from the boats, thus floating the boats full of men easily to the beach. By midnight, more than 10,000 Union troops were on Roanoke Island. Nearly seventy ships waited in the distant blackness. The area around the harbor was filled with soldiers starting small fires to stay warm. Roanoke's undefended southern end was fully occupied by the North.

The 200 Confederate spies quietly made their way back to their small fort in the middle of the island, where 200 others were waiting. Did any of them sleep that night, knowing 10,000 Union soldiers would be coming their way in the morning?

At dawn on February 8, the Union troops started their march to the interior of the island. Advancing along the island's only road, the Twenty-fifth Massachusetts was the first troop to come upon the Confederates' redoubt and the cannon fire coming from it. The men of the Twenty-fifth Massachusetts fired their muskets toward the redoubt, spread themselves flat to the ground to reload, then jumped up again to fire. Wounded Union soldiers were passed to the back of the line and sent on to the hospitals set up in two family homes at Ashby's Harbor. Other Union troops were coming at the redoubt from the right and left, plodding slowly through thick, soupy marsh to get there. Hearing the Federals closing in from the sides, the 400 Confederates abandoned their fort and retreated, running up the road toward their forts on the north end of the island.

Confederate couriers ran the news of the approaching Union troops to the forts on the north end. But the Roanoke Island Confederates were unprepared for an inland fight. Their cannons were pointed toward the sound.

Lieutenant Colonel Fowle of the Thirty-first North Carolina carried the flag of surrender. The Union troops secured the camps and forts and went about the island capturing prisoners. The prisoners included nearly 800 men from a regiment that had arrived in response to General Wise's plea for reinforcements to help the Confederates on Roanoke Island. They were just in time to be captured by the Union.

The official tally for the day showed that twenty-three Confederate soldiers were killed, with fifty-eight more wounded, sixty-two missing, and over 2,000 captured as prisoners. On the Union side, only twenty-seven were killed, with 214 wounded and thirteen missing.

The Union soldiers foraged the island and watched over their prisoners. One Union soldier wrote: "The prisoners are a motley set, all clothed (I can hardly say uniformed) in a dirty homespun looking gray cloth. I should think every man's suit was cut from a design of his own. Their head covering was in unison with the rest of their rig, from stovepipe hats to coonskin caps; with everything for blankets, from old bed quilts, cotton bagging, strips of carpet to buffalo robes."

Burnside had complete control of the island and all of its assets. He then set out to destroy the Mosquito Fleet, a task he soon completed. He ordered his assistants to obtain oaths of allegiance to the Union from the Roanoke Island natives, which many natives actually took. Burnside took over the Confederate forts and renamed them Fort Foster, Fort Reno, and Fort Parke. He sent the prisoners to a camp in Elizabeth City, North Carolina, to exchange for Union prisoners.

The Roanoke Island capture proved valuable for Burnside. Within months, he had also taken over the North Carolina coastal towns of Edenton, Winton, New Bern, Morehead City, Beaufort, as well as Fort Macon to the south. Roanoke Island remained a Union stronghold for the duration of the war, with troops stationed there until the spring of 1867.

Freedom Found
· 1862 ·

Whispers circulated among the slaves of the Outer Banks and eastern North Carolina: The Yankees had control of Roanoke Island. With the news came a glimmer of hope that they might actually someday find freedom.

The first escaped slaves arrived just a few days after General Ambrose Burnside's men had won the battle securing Roanoke Island for the Union on February 8, 1862. Twenty men, women, and children reached Roanoke Island in a small dinghy after a long journey down the Chowan River and across 35 miles of the open Albemarle Sound. Their masters had fired shotguns at them as they escaped a nearby community on the mainland, but they had made it to safer ground. Landing on the sandy beach at the north end of Roanoke Island, the runaway slaves were met by a Union soldier and led to General Burnside's tent.

General Burnside allowed the runaway slaves to stay on the island. After writing down their names, their former masters' names, and places of residence, he gave them jobs and supplies. Best of all, he promised not to return them to their "owners."

It didn't take long for word to get around: Roanoke Island was an asylum, a place where slaves were free. The immigration to Roanoke began. Within a month, between seventy and eighty refugee slaves, most of them from the mainland communities of Elizabeth City, Plymouth, and Edenton, escaped their masters and traveled across the sounds to Roanoke Island. The former slaves congregated in a small camp near the outskirts of the Union soldiers' camp, where Burnside let them inhabit the barracks and buildings of a former Confederate camp. The freedmen, as they were known, were paid to work for the Union soldiers, washing clothes, cooking, chopping wood, carrying supplies from boats to the camp, and doing whatever else anyone needed them to do.

The former slaves quickly organized a community of their own. They built two churches out of pine trees and branches and supplies they had salvaged from the Union camp. Refugee Martha Culling opened a community school in a small building near the Union camp. By early April, there were approximately 250 people in the refugee settlement, and the freedmen were building a new life of their own.

Soon, however, there were so many runaway slaves on Roanoke Island that the small refugee camp was overflowing. The freedmen did what was necessary to make room for everyone who came, but the Union authorities began to worry about the overcrowded conditions. They were concerned about improper sanitation and diseases, as well as the way the overcrowding at the barracks might affect the Union camp.

To take control of the situation and allow the slaves to remain on the island, General Burnside created an officially sanctioned contraband camp, similar to others that harbored escaped slaves on Union-controlled lands in the South. He briefly put Post Commandant Rush Hawkins in charge of employing the refugees and distributing supplies and clothing among them. It didn't take long, however, for the Union to decide to give control of the refugee camp to someone outside of the military. They created a position—Superintendent of the Poor in the Department of North Carolina—and gave the job to a man named Vincent Colyer, who was ordered to feed, clothe, shelter, and employ not only the freedmen on Roanoke Island but also the 10,000 freedmen in North Carolina.

On Roanoke Island, Colyer employed the former slaves to work on Fort Burnside and build docks on the island. The freedmen also worked as carpenters, blacksmiths, launderers, and cooks for the Union soldiers, as well as continuing to improve their own small community. Though conditions were not always perfect, they were amazed to find themselves with jobs that paid and opportunities for education, marriage, and worship.

President Lincoln's Emancipation Proclamation in January 1863 brought a new wave of refugees to Roanoke Island. Now there were more than a thousand former slaves congregated on the north end of the island, their population more than doubling that of the native islanders.

In May of 1863, a new Superintendent of the Poor in the Department of North Carolina, the Reverend Horace James, was appointed. James was a well-educated minister who strongly opposed slavery and believed that the freedmen could one day fully support themselves. James had high hopes for making the Roanoke Island colony self-sufficient, with the colonists eventually making a living in agriculture, fishing, and manufacturing. James believed that Roanoke Island was the perfect place for such a colony, as it was safely protected by water on all sides and it had suitable soil, good water, dense forest, and a variety of natural resources. James went North to raise money and materials for the colony. He passionately pled with the Northerners to support a "New Social Order in the South," and raised $8,000.

While James was raising money, in mid-June of 1863, Brigadier General Edward A. Wild came to Roanoke Island to recruit freedmen to fight for the Union cause. Wild had orders to recruit all of the able-bodied men on the island and to help Reverend James organize the Roanoke Island Freedmen's Colony for the wives, children, aged and infirm that would be left behind when the men left for battle. Wild took control of unoccupied lands on the island and laid them out in lots for the freedmen. Joseph Williams, a freedman who was helping Wild, noted that Wild "established a colony there for the support of the wives of the soldiers of his brigade, and also homes for the old and young and those who are not fit for service." Wild also gave the freed slaves boats and schooners that had been captured from the Confederates and helped them build more buildings.

The Roanoke Island Freedmen's Colony consisted of about 1,100 acres near the former Confederate barracks. The colony stretched from Weir's Point to Pork's Point on the northwest end of the island, near the present-day Dare County Regional Airport. James and Wild laid out streets and avenues and gave away large lots that could accommodate both a house and a garden.

For the freed slaves, becoming landowners was a dream come true. The freedmen eagerly cleared the trees, briars, and overgrowth from their lots and built their own houses with only hand tools and scavenged lumber. James wrote of the scene, "they are so animated by the prospect of a homestead of their own, and the little comforts of a freehold, that they labor, every spare moment by night as well as day, and are as happy as larks in their toil."

In the fall of 1863, the colony was making good progress. James had recruited missionaries from the North, mostly single women, to educate the colonists and help with the distribution of supplies.

Meanwhile, Wild and his black recruits, fighting their way through the South, sent boatloads of women and children to Roanoke Island, some with their baggage, horses, and carts and some with nothing at all but the clothes on their backs. Their numbers completely overwhelmed the Roanoke Island colony. By January 1864 there were nearly 3,000 freedmen on the island, with nowhere to spend the cold winter months. The barracks were packed as full as possible. There were people living in small mud and brush huts in the woods. Sanitation was poor.

There was only one doctor on the whole island, for both soldiers and freedmen, and an outbreak of small-pox appeared in January 1864. Crucial supplies weren't making it to the island, probably being sold on the black market somewhere along the route. The missionaries complained about their dire need for clothing, food, and supplies.

Mercifully, the colonists got through the winter of 1864, and James considered the colony a success, providing "a safe and undisturbed retreat for the families of soldiers, who were nobly defending our flag at Petersburg, Charleston, and Wilmington." He cited the construction of more than 500 homes, the instruction of hundreds of children, the introduction of manufacturing facilities and stores for trade, and the expansion of fisheries. James established a saw mill on the island, which brought great prospects of employment and prosperity.

But all was not as blissful as James made it out to be. Letters from the missionaries to their northern missionary associations revealed problems, such as a serious lack of supplies, especially clothing, and mistreatment by the military. The Union military, they said, didn't pay the civilian workers properly, and some people hadn't been paid for years. Even with these blights on the living situation, the colonists and the missionaries remained true to their task of maintaining the community.

The Roanoke Island Freedmen's Colony thrived until the war ended, but, alas, it was not to last. Promises made to the freedmen were not upheld. The colonists believed that the plots of land given to them were theirs to keep, since they had no reason to believe otherwise. But after the war, the former owners claimed the Freedmen's Colony land and demanded it back. Those who could prove ownership were given their land, leaving many of the black freedmen homeless. In addition, the government discontinued rations to the colonists. Many of the freedmen could no longer support themselves on the island.

Over time, the majority of the Roanoke Island freedmen were transported to freedmen's colonies on the mainland. The hopes for a permanent colony of freed slaves on Roanoke Island and a "New Social Order for the South" were dashed. By the end of the decade, only 300 former slaves remained on the island. These freedmen worked, raised families, bought their own land, and established a neighborhood known as California in the center of the island. Descendants of the Freedman's Colony live on Roanoke Island to this day.

Though no structural traces of the original colony remain today, there are memorials to the colonists on the north end of the island. The Roanoke Island Freedom Colony Memorial is at the intersection of Airport and Old County Roads, where many of the freedmen are believed to be buried, and the National Park Service also has a monument, "First Light of Freedom," on the Fort Raleigh National Historic Site.

A Glow in the Darkness
· 1896 ·

Richard Etheridge, keeper of U.S. Life-Saving Station 17 at Pea Island, noted the change in the weather. Yesterday's heavy southwest wind had developed into an even stronger northeast gale and was now worrying the seas into froth. The skies darkened, the barometer reading dropped, and rain began to fall.

A bulletin from the Weather Bureau confirmed his fears, and soon the telephone wire was alive with calls from the other keepers stationed at various points along the Outer Banks. A hurricane was spinning toward the Outer Banks; Etheridge promptly noted the information in his logbook on October 10, 1896, and returned to his duties managing the station's crew of surfmen. It was their duty to watch for shipwrecks in this storm—and to rescue any survivors.

By the next day, the storm surge was tremendous. The surfmen at Station 16, Oregon Inlet, abandoned their station when it was nearly washed out to sea. In some places, ocean water washed clear across the banks to the sound, sweeping houses off their foundations and livestock out to sea. The water was so high that there was no beach to speak of; only the tops of the highest dunes rose above the water.

Etheridge was forced to do something he rarely did—call off his station's regular beach patrol. Every night for the past fourteen years, like clockwork, his crew of six surfmen had walked their assigned stretches of Pea Island between the Oregon Inlet station and New Inlet, scanning the sea for ships in trouble. But tonight they would not go. Tonight the crow's nest atop their station would have to do for a lookout.

The surfmen took turns standing in the station's high perch, scanning the dark sea with rain driving into their eyes, holding on for dear life in the whipping winds. Life was hard in the Life-Saving Service, but the work of saving shipwreck victims was rewarding and it was one of the few steady jobs on the Outer Banks. Endless solitary patrols along the beach, rescues in the worst of elements, battling with the merciless Atlantic, and long months away from family were the tradeoffs for regular government pay.

The crew at Pea Island may have appreciated their Life-Saving Service jobs a little more than the men at other stations. This was the only place in the South where seven black men had the same opportunities and the same pay as white men, even though to get it they had to be segregated from white men completely.

The Pea Island Lifesaving Station was the first and only all-black Lifesaving Station in the nation, and Etheridge was the nation's only black keeper. The fact that they were in their positions at all was a miracle in the postbellum South. Before Etheridge, the highest rank black men had ever achieved in the Life-Saving Service were the lowest jobs available in the stations. But Etheridge, a former slave, had managed the unthinkable accomplishment of becoming keeper in 1880.

In the Station 17 crow's nest during the dark night of the 1896 hurricane, Surfman Theodore Meekins thought he saw a red glow in the darkness. He wasn't sure what he had seen, so he summoned Etheridge, who ordered the firing of a bright rocket flare. They waited, wondering what would unfold.

When a faint glow of response came from the south, Etheridge and Meekins raced out of the observation tower, and all seven crewmen hurried into familiar action, scrambling into oilskins, dragging out the beach carts, and hitching up the mules. After the carts were ready, they gathered their supplies, including ropes and lines, the sand anchor, the breeches buoy, the Lyle gun, the medical kit, blankets, flares, and shovels.

The trip south along the flooded beach was painfully slow. The men used all of their might to get the carts and mules down the beach in the dark, not knowing what scene they would soon find or what strength it would require. All of the stations, including Pea Island, had been through times when mistakes were made and lives were lost. Every surfman, white and black, had at one time doubted his skills, and every surfman had shared in the joy of saving lives. Which would this night bring?

Two miles and two hours later, the crew saw what they had come to find: a broken, three-masted schooner keeled over on the inner sandbar, about 50 yards from shore, with nearly a dozen people clinging to its rigging. The people on the masts shouted with joy at the sight of the approaching men.

The lifesaving crew knew what needed to be done, but they couldn't do it. Because the beach was washed over, they couldn't set up the breeches buoy, ground the anchor, or put the Lyle gun in place. Their lifesaving equipment was useless without any hard ground, and they had purposefully left their boat behind at the station, knowing the sea was too wild to use it.

Meanwhile, the ship was breaking apart, its flotsam knocking at the knees of the impotent surfmen, while its passengers grew too weak to hold themselves in the rigging.

It was Etheridge's idea to have surfmen swim out to the ship, but he didn't have to order them to do it: Theodore Meekins and Stanley Wise volunteered to go. The crew tied a line around the two men's waists and sent them forward into the rabid surf. After an exhausting swim through the jumble of floating wreckage, they reached the schooner and tied a line to it. The surfmen on the shore held the line taut while Meekins and Wise shimmied along it with the youngest shipwreck victim, the captain's three-year-old son, and came to safer ground.

Nine trips into the sea were made that night, with two surfmen at a time making their way out and back in, rescuing the captain's wife, the crew and, finally, Captain Sylvester Gardiner. (It's said that Theodore Meekins went out all nine times.) In less than an hour, the crew of the Pea Island station completed their task. The *E.S. Newman* schooner was gone, but not a single life was lost, and the surfmen must have felt the warm glow of success.

The Pea Island lifesavers carried the captain, his family, and crew back to the Pea Island Station, where they gave them medical treatment, fresh clothes, coffee, beds, and blankets. Keeper Etheridge gave up his own quarters so the lady and her child could have some privacy from all the men in the small station.

As the shipwreck victims drifted off to sleep that night, were any of them, for even a moment, re-thinking their country's racial inequalities? After all, they were nine white people rescued by and staying in the only station in the entire Life-Saving Service that was staffed entirely by blacks. And it was, after all, 1896, when race was still very much an issue among Americans in the South, despite the outcome of the Civil War.

No one knows what went through the minds of the white shipwreck victims that night, but it is known that Captain Gardiner was grateful. In the days that followed, he wandered the beach looking for remnants of his ship and cargo. When he found the ship's nameplate he presented it to the surfmen, who in turn gave it to Theodore Meekins.

The nameplate was the only recognition given to the Pea Island men. Undoubtedly Etheridge must have felt that his men deserved medals for the uncommonly brave act of venturing into the highest Atlantic tides recorded in fifty years to successfully rescue an entire ship's crew. His surfmen had gone far beyond the call of duty. But in the end the medals didn't come. One of the bravest acts in the history of the Life-Saving Service, and the Pea Island crew's greatest achievement, went unrecognized.

The crew at Pea Island saved lives for another fifty-one years, continuing long after Etheridge's death in 1900, and the transference of the Life-Saving Service to the U.S. Coast Guard. The station was decommissioned in 1947. It wasn't until a hundred years after the wreck of the *E.S. Newman* that the Pea Island Life-Saving Station crew got the full recognition it deserved. In 1996, the Coast Guard posthumously awarded Richard Etheridge and the crew of the station—Theodore Meekins, William Irving, Lewis Wescott, Stanley Wise, Benjamin Bowser, and Dorman Pugh—the Gold Life-Saving Medal, its highest peacetime honor.

Roughing It at Kitty Hawk

• 1900 •

Wilbur Wright read the letter from Captain William Tate again. "In answering I would say that you would find here nearly any type of ground you could wish; you could, for instance, get a stretch of sandy land 1 mile by 5 with a bare hill in the center 80 feet high, not a tree or bush anywhere to break the evenness of the wind current. This in my opinion would be a fine place; our winds are always steady, generally, from 10 to 20 miles velocity per hour."

Wright had to agree with Tate. The area he described, a fishing village called Kitty Hawk on the remote Outer Banks of North Carolina, seemed like a fine place for him and his brother Orville to experiment with their flying machines. They had a few basic requirements for their task, including open space without trees, preferably without a large population nearby; soft, sandy soil for landings; and strong, steady winds. Tate seemed to be describing a location that met their conditions better than any other place they had considered.

Tate's letter, dated August 18, 1900, advised the brothers not to wait too late in the fall to come to Kitty Hawk. "The autumn generally gets a little rough by Nov.," his letter said. Tate told the brothers they would find telegraph communication and mail service at Kitty Hawk, as well as a place to pitch tents and the option to take meals with a local family. "If you decide to try your machine here & come I will take pleasure in doing all I can for your convenience & success & pleasure, & I assure you you will find a hospitable people when you come among us," Tate wrote. The letter made the decision easy. The Wright brothers would go to Kitty Hawk.

The two brothers, the sons of a well-to-do bishop, were city born and bred. They had no idea what they were in for on the outer reaches of North Carolina. From their comfortable home in Dayton, Ohio, they could not have imagined the conditions in which they would soon find themselves.

Less than a month later, Wilbur Wright left Dayton and traveled to Elizabeth City, North Carolina. He had missed the weekly mail boat to Kitty Hawk by one day, so he hired a local man, Captain Israel Perry, to sail him across the Albemarle Sound. On this schooner trip, Wright got his first taste of Outer Banks weather. What should have taken only part of a day turned into a harrowing, two-day adventure of "storms and terrors by day & by night, of privations of hunger and thirst, of bloodthirsty beasts, etc., etc.," Wright later wrote to his family. In addition, Wright was appalled at the unsanitary condition of Perry's galley; he ate only a jar of jelly his sister had given him throughout the entire two-day trip.

Well dressed in a suit and hat, Wright finally landed on the marshy shores of Kitty Hawk Bay on September 13, 1900. Young Elijah Baum greeted him at the docks and led him directly to William Tate's house.

The Tates welcomed Wright into their home, offering him a breakfast of ham and eggs. Wright boarded with them until his brother arrived later in the month. Wright found himself in a very different, much more primitive world than the one he had grown up in. He wrote home to his family about the simplicity of the Tate home, like all other homes in the area, which he described as "a two-story frame with unplanned siding, not painted, no plaster on the walls." Wright marveled that the home had no adornments like carpets, pictures, or books.

"There is little wealth and no luxurious living," he wrote to his family of the Kitty Hawkers, but he added, "They are friendly and neighborly and I think there is rarely any real suffering among them."

Orville arrived in Kitty Hawk with the glider equipment on September 28, and the two found a high place south of the village to set up camp. During their first weeks of experiments, the brothers got plenty of what they had wanted: that steady Outer Banks wind. On one occasion, continuous 30 miles per hour winds kept them trapped inside the tent for two days. "Wednesday morning the Kitty Hawkers were out early peering around the edge of the woods and out of their upstair windows to see whether our camp was still in existence," Orville wrote to his sister in October.

Though they found time to experiment, the Wright brothers were frustrated with the winds because they were extreme— too strong one day, then too mild the next. Orville described it to his family:

> About two or three times a week we have to crawl up at ten or eleven o'clock to hold the tent down. . . . When we crawl out of the tent to fix things outside the sand fairly blinds us. It blows across the ground in clouds. We certainly can't complain of the place. We came down here for wind and sand, and we have got them.

And in the fall on the Outer Banks, even the tent was not the coziest place to be, as Orville described in one of his letters:

> We each of us have two blankets, but I 'most freeze every night. The wind blows in on my head and I pull the blankets up over my head, when my feet freeze, I reverse the process. I keep this up all night. . . .

The Wright brothers had been forewarned about the Outer Banks winds, so their discomfort was not totally unexpected. Their main distress was one they had not anticipated: the lack of their accustomed foods. "Our pantry in its most depleted state would be a mammoth affair compared with the Kitty Hawk stores," wrote Orville. Wilbur and Orville subsisted mostly on canned goods, eggs, biscuits, and tomatoes. Occasionally a local would offer them some fish or fowl. Bacon, meat, butter, and milk were rare treats, as Orville described to his sister in a letter:

> I have just stopped a minute to eat a spoonful of condensed milk. No one down here has any regular milk. The poor cows have such a hard time scraping up a living that they don't have any time for making milk. You never saw such pitiable looking creatures as the horses, hogs and cows are down here. The only things that grow fat are the bedbugs, mosquitoes, and wood ticks. . . .

The Kitty Hawkers caught, killed, or grew most of their food and supplemented what they obtained themselves with a few items from the stores. On the other hand, the Wright brothers wanted to buy all their food, and this fact upset the economic balance in town.

Yet for any of their discomforts, the Wright brothers grew to like the Outer Banks. Their first glider experiments were successful, and they found beauty beyond the comforts of home. Orville wrote to his sister:

> The sunsets here are the prettiest I have ever seen. The clouds light up in all colors, in the background, with deep blue clouds of various shapes fringed with gold before. The moon rises in much the same style, and lights up this pile of sand almost like day.

The brothers returned to Dayton, but in 1901 they returned to Kitty Hawk in the summer instead of the fall, in hopes of encountering more moderate but steady winds. They set up camp farther south of Kitty Hawk village, near the Kill Devil Hills, and erected crude buildings to house themselves and other scientists who came to experiment with them. But on this trip, instead of cold and extreme winds, they were greeted by mosquitoes. Orville wrote about it in a letter:

Mr. Huffaker arrived Thursday afternoon, and with him a swarm of mosquitoes which came in a mighty cloud, almost darkening the sun. This was the beginning of the most miserable existence I have ever passed through. The agonies of typhoid fever with its attending starvation are as nothing in comparison. . . . The sand and the grass and trees and hills and everything was fairly covered with them. They chewed us clear through our underwear and "socks." Lumps began swelling up all over my body like hen's eggs. . . . Misery! Misery!

Despite the hardships of Outer Banks living, Kitty Hawk and the Kill Devil Hills proved to be the perfect locations for testing and perfecting the flying machines. The Wright brothers returned in the fall of 1902 and again in September 1903.

The Wrights survived the Outer Banks' tests of their perseverance and were rewarded with success. After four years of experimenting and enduring harsh conditions, on December 17, 1903, the Wright brothers did what they had come to do. The winds that morning were strong—20 to 25 miles per hour out of the north and cold—but they lifted the 1903 Wright Flyer over the sands of Kill Devil Hills. The machine flew four times that day, the longest flight lasting fifty-seven seconds and covering 852 feet.

Before the Wrights could flee the Outer Banks, anxious to get home to the comforts of Christmas in Dayton, the wind played a final prank on the brothers. Back at camp after the flights a strong gust lifted one wing of the aircraft, rolling it head over heels away from camp. By the time the brothers were able to reach it, the craft had been damaged beyond repair. They didn't even bother to fix it. They were packed up and ready to go two days later.

In the same place where the Wright brothers flew the world's first airplane—as well as battled mosquitoes, shivered in the cold, and staved off hunger—a monument was constructed in 1932, known as the Wright Brothers National Memorial. The memorial honors the Wright brothers' accomplishments that were "conceived by genius and achieved by dauntless resolution and unconquerable faith."

The First Music on the Airwaves

· 1902 ·

The Albemarle Sound was particularly rough that January morning in 1901, and Captain Chiseltine struggled to keep his schooner on course to Roanoke Island. One of his passengers, Mr. Thiessen, was horribly seasick, a condition worsened by the overwhelming odor of a large wheel of Limburger cheese brought on board by the other passenger, Mr. Reginald A. Fessenden. Fessenden, working for the U.S. Weather Bureau, had insisted on accompanying the schooner's cargo of Bureau equipment from Cobb Island, Maryland, to Roanoke Island. He would not be separated from his equipment, even if it meant traveling by sea in this storm rather than taking the safer route through Norfolk with his wife and son. The red-headed Fessenden, though rather quick-tempered and domineering it seemed to the captain, made a surprising offer to hang the Limburger over the side of the boat, in an effort to ease his associate's condition.

The day's storm worsened, the seas swelled, and Captain Chiseltine professed the schooner to be in danger. The unwieldy objects the schooner was towing for Fessenden—two 50-foot mastlike wooden posts—dragged and swashed in the water until the captain found the boat unmanageable. "We'll have to set them adrift," he told his passengers. "Absolutely not," replied Fessenden.

But later, when another squall rocked the ship, Captain Chiseltine ignored Fessenden's wishes and tried to set the posts free in an effort to steady the ship. A scuffle ensued between the two men over the issue, but the posts remained where they were. Luckily, the wind soon subsided somewhat and another schooner came on the scene to help out. The journey to Roanoke Island continued, and the posts and passengers arrived safely at the town docks.

Fessenden met his wife, Helen, and son, Ken, in Manteo. They booked accommodations at the Tranquil House Inn, the larger of the two hotels in town, paying to occupy an entire up-stairs wing. The Fessendens spread their belongings among several rooms, allowing for an office, dining room, bedrooms, and sitting room.

Fessenden, former chief chemist for Thomas Edison and an inventor and pioneer in the field of wireless telegraphy, was on the island to work. The U.S. Weather Bureau, which had several stations along the Outer Banks, hired him in hopes of inventing a way to quickly communicate weather data to ships at sea. The previous month, on December 23, 1900, Fessenden had made history when he had transmitted his own voice 1 mile between two Weather Bureau towers on Cobb Island. "One, two, three, four. Is it snowing where you are, Mr. Thiessen?" he had asked his assistant. It was the first time the human voice had ever been transferred from one place to an-other without the benefit of wires. The Weather Bureau had high hopes for Fessenden's future inventions and moved him to the Outer Banks to further his research.

To assist Fessenden in his experiments, two 50-foot tow-ers were erected on the Outer Banks, using the posts that Fes-senden had saved during his journey. One was erected on the northwest end of Roanoke Island (near the foot of today's Croatan Sound Bridge). The other was raised on Hatteras Island in Buxton (the site of the present-day Fessenden Recreation Center), along with a small outpost laboratory just big enough to house equipment and a technician. A third tower was erected in Cape Henry, Virginia. Electronic equipment was mounted on top of the poles.

Fessenden chose the Roanoke Island tower as his headquarters and had a small laboratory built there. Helen Fessenden recounted in her book about her husband:

> Directly after breakfast, the men would start off in a rickety conveyance for the Wireless Station which had been located on the west side of the island. They took sandwiches with them and brewed coffee at lunch time. Home again about six and after supper two or three hours of office work, correspondence, patent applications, official Weather Bureau returns and accounts.

Fessenden's full schedule also included traveling between the three stations, taking boats across the inlets and sounds, and riding in horse and buggy up and down the long, sandy stretch of Hatteras Island. Men were hired to staff the outposts and Roanoke Island stations and to help Fessenden experiment with transmitting messages. Fessenden spent the entire year of 1901 conducting experiments between the three stations. Knowing that others were working with the similar technology in other parts of the world at the same time as he was, Fessenden was driven by a need to be the first to discover new ways to work in the field of wireless technology. "In 1902," wrote Helen Fessenden, "storm clouds began to gather everywhere, general as well as personal, and wireless work speeded up to an almost frenzied tempo."

Fessenden's hard work paid off. A March 28, 1902, letter to his patent attorney, Mr. Wolcott, reported the following success:

> What do you say to a receiver which gives telegrams at the rate of a thousand words per minute and is so

sensitive that it gives that rate when the coherer will not even give a click and when the coherer cannot be read when the power is increased over ten times, i.e., when measurement shows works at this rate with less than ten per cent of the power necessary to work the coherer at all. Also that it is perfectly positive and gives these results in its very crudest form and on the very first trial?

Well, this is what I have now and what I have been working over the Hatteras-Roanoke line, as fast as the man could handle the key. So it is no theory but an accomplished fact.

Less than a week later, Fessenden wrote to Wolcott again, this time with more good news:

I have more good news for you. You remember I telephoned about a mile in 1900—but thought it would take too much power to telephone across the Atlantic. Well I can now telephone as far as I can telegraph, which is across the Pacific Ocean if desired. I have sent varying musical notes from Hatteras and received them here [Roanoke Island] with but 3 watts of energy, and they were very loud and plain, i.e., as loud as in any ordinary telephone. . . . The new receiver is a wonder!!!

Thus, the first musical notes ever transported over radio waves were sent 50 miles across the Pamlico and Roanoke sounds, from a small wireless station antenna in Buxton to an antenna on Roanoke Island. It was a breakthrough that would lead to the world's first radio broadcast, but not right away.

There was a great deal of interest in Fessenden's discovery, both from the government and the private sector. But Fessenden and the Weather Bureau argued over the patents, with the result that no one could benefit from his work for quite some time. Fessenden's superior in the Weather Bureau wanted a share of the patents even though Fessenden had done all the work. When Fessenden balked, his superior took away all his worthy assistants, making his experiments nearly impossible. The situation deteriorated to the point that Fessenden left the Weather Bureau in August 1902 to conduct his research elsewhere

With Fessenden gone, the Weather Bureau continued experiments for a short time. However, no one had nearly the knowledge or experience of Fessenden, and before long the Weather Bureau gave up and sold his equipment at auction. Fessenden, backed by wealthy businessmen, continued his experiments in Massachusetts.

On Christmas Eve 1906, from Brant Rock, Massachusetts, Fessenden made history again, broadcasting the world's first entertainment over the airwaves. For this historic moment, he played a recording of Handel's "Largo" on an Ediphone, performed "O Holy Night" live on the violin himself, and read a Christmas message from the Bible. Wireless radio operators at sea, accustomed to hearing only the dots and dashes of Morse code, were shocked.

Fessenden was well known among his peers, but he never became a household name, probably because he had a hard time maneuvering in the business world. Italian physicist Guglielmo Marconi is commonly credited with development of wireless telegraphy, for it was he who first sent dot-and-dash messages over the airwaves in 1895. But by the time Fessenden sent the musical notes over the airwaves of the Outer Banks, Marconi's system had not progressed much further than coded messages over short distances. Fessenden's system carried voice and music and was much more influential on today's radio broadcasting. Later Fessenden achieved two-way voice transmission by radio across the Atlantic, between Scotland and Massachusetts. Fessenden made many other discoveries and inventions in his life, including the fathometer (depth finder), the wireless compass, a turbo-electric drive for battleships, and submarine signaling devices.

Fessenden was only on the Outer Banks for less than two years, and this brief episode could have easily been forgotten. However, the Outer Banks remembers Fessenden and honors him with a roadside marker in Buxton and the naming of the county's senior center, on the same site as Fessenden's Hatteras outpost, as the Fessenden Center. Other evidence of Fessenden's presence exists on Roanoke Island near the base of the Croatan Sound Bridge leading from Roanoke Island to Mann's Harbor. At low tide, about 300 yards offshore, you can see a large concrete slab protruding from the water. This was the foundation of Fessenden's Roanoke Island work station.

Mystery on Diamond Shoals

· 1921 ·

There she sat—stranded hard on the shoals and surrounded by walls of breakers—a magnificent five-masted schooner more than 250 feet in length, her massive sails fully set and snapping in the wind. A beautiful, unreachable mystery ship, the name of which no one even knew.

She was first spotted on Diamond Shoals at dawn on the morning of January 31, 1921. Surfman C. P. Brady was on the morning watch at the Cape Hatteras Coast Guard Station, looking through the telescope into the misty morning over the ocean. At first he couldn't believe his eyes. She seemed to appear out of nowhere. But she was really there, hard aground with no signs of survivors.

No boat could reach her, but plenty tried.

Surfmen from the Creed's Hill and Big Kinnakeet Coast Guard stations met the Cape Hatteras crew on the beach as they tried to launch their surfboat into the ocean. They struggled to get two boats past the breakers to reach the boat that first day but could only get within a half-mile of the ship, too far away to read her name. All anyone could see was that she was shoaled in "in a boiling bed of breakers," as Big Kinnakeet's keeper, C. R. Hooper, would later put it. What was eerie was that she seemed to have been abandoned. There was no sign of life, no crew member signaling or calling for help. A ladder was hanging over the side, and the lifeboats were missing from their holds.

The next day the Coast Guard cutter *Seminole* arrived from Wilmington, North Carolina, and the Cape Hatteras station keeper, Baxter Miller, and some crew members went out with a boat to meet it. But still, the ocean was too rough to reach the ship, which by then had breakers crashing over its decks. The *Seminole* anchored a mile away and awaited the ocean's calming, which was not soon in coming. Another day brought the departure of the *Seminole* due to mechanical difficulties and the arrival of the Coast Guard cutter *Manning* from Norfolk. The *Manning* brought with it a tug, the *Rescue,* from a salvage company, to use if there was anything left to salvage after Diamond Shoals was through with her. However, even three days later no vessel could approach the ship enshrouded by white water.

The days of waiting to identify the ship created an air of curiosity and intrigue not only around the station but also off the island. What in the world was this ship doing on the shoals under full sail? Where was the crew? The *Ledger Dispatch* in Norfolk posed these same questions on its front page.

Finally, on February 4, the seas calmed. The *Manning* made calls in an attempt to rouse any survivors on the ship but there was no response. It was the *Rescue* that approached the stranded ship and learned her name. She was the *Carroll A. Deering,* hailing from Bath, Maine, due at port in Norfolk several days ago.

The *Rescue's* captain, James Carlson, and his four men motored a small boat from their anchored tug to the massive ship and boarded via a rope that was left hanging over the side. The sails were shredded, the decks empty, ocean water swashed in the hold, loose halyards dangled in the wind. Stranger still was the sight down below. The galley was set for a meal—pea soup, a pan of spareribs, and a pot of coffee on the stove. The captain's trunk was missing and charts were strewn over his floor. Several crew members' boots were on the floor of the captain's room. The steering gear was ruined, the rudder disengaged, the binnacle box smashed. No one could find the captain's log or the nautical instruments.

The *Rescue*'s men took a few items from the ship, including the sails, flags, chairs, lights, and the bell. They took the captain's Bible to return to his family and rescued three cats, the only known survivors of the wreck of the *Carroll A. Deering*. Captain Carlson said the ship itself could not be salvaged since she was grounded too hard in the shoals and her keel buried fourteen feet deep in the sand.

The story of the *Carroll A. Deering*'s final voyage is studded with oddities. She was launched at Bath, Maine, in 1919 by the G. G. Deering Company. In August of 1919 she had cleared Hampton Roads, Virginia, bound for Rio de Janeiro, but ended up in Lewes, Delaware, a week later. The captain was ill and wanted off the ship. Besides, he had told some people in Norfolk that he didn't like or trust the ship's ten-man crew. They found a new captain to make the trip to Rio, Captain Willis B. Wormell of Maine.

The *Carroll A. Deering* eventually made it to Rio de Janeiro with its load of coal and left for the return journey on December 2, 1920, with no return cargo. She made one stop on the way back home, in Barbados, West Indies.

On January 23, 1921, the Light Vessel on Frying Pan Shoals on the southern coast of North Carolina reported the *Deering* passing by in good weather. But then something strange happened. For some reason she didn't pass Cape Lookout on the central North Carolina coast, only 90 miles north, until a week later, at 4:30 P.M. on January 29. Granted, there had been a gale at sea for two days, but the ship should have made far better time than that. That trip should have taken twelve hours or less. The engineer on the Light Vessel at Lookout Shoals took a photo of the impressive ship and noted some oddities about its passing. The crew, he said, were scattered about the decks with no discipline whatsoever, and there were even crewmembers on the quarterdeck, typically the captain's area alone. It was a red-headed sailor with a foreign accent, not the captain, who contacted the Light Vessel. "We've lost both anchors and chains in the gale of Frying Pan Shoals—forward word to our owners," he said to them through the megaphone. But the ship was under control and under sail at the time. Two days later she was found on Diamond Shoals, not a soul aboard but those three cats.

The *Carroll A. Deering* sat out on the shoals for nearly two weeks. On Valentine's Day, twelve local men took four sailboats out to the wreck to claim what they could. They salvaged a lot of goods the Outer Bankers could use, but they said it seemed like the ship had already been plundered. Things were missing that should have been there, like personal belongings of the crew. They got everything back to shore and had a big sale in Hatteras Village, under Wreck Commissioner W. L. Gaskill's watch. The locals bought up all the food, including meats, coffee, spices, peas and beans, mustard, grits, pumpkins, tomatoes, peppers, molasses, milk, prunes, lard, sugar and flour. Also salvaged and sold were the furnishings and other items, such as tables, chairs, desks, trunks, bed frames, lanterns, lamps, mattresses, brooms, blankets, pillows, hoses, twine, rope, charts, boxes, and more. Three weeks later the Coast Guard dynamited the ship because she was a navigational hazard. The locals snapped up all the boards that washed ashore to use in building projects around the island. A good section of her bow and capstan washed ashore on Ocracoke Island.

A huge investigation followed and was played out in the newspapers. The lifeboats were never found and no one from the crew ever turned up anywhere. And the story just got stranger and stranger.

There were rumors of mutiny, of the captain being murdered at sea. It seems the First Mate Charles McLellan picked a fight with the captain during their layover in Barbados. The captain of another ship overheard McLellan threaten Wormell, saying "I'll kill you before it's all over, old man." Wormell ordered him off the ship and the crew went on a five-day drinking binge. McLellan was even thrown in jail for some drunken act. Wormell complained to other boat captains about his first mate and his unruly crew. But eventually the crew returned and the *Deering* left Barbados on January 9, 1921, headed for Norfolk, Virginia. Adding to this theory of mutiny was the fact that the captain's handwriting was no longer on the ocean charts after January 23.

There were suspicions that the crew had been involved in smuggling rum from the Caribbean (it was during Prohibition after all) and that they had boarded another ship and intentionally grounded the *Deering*. If they were trying to steer off the shoals, people said, they would have brought down the sails. There were theories that Russian pirates had taken over the ship. The engineer at the Cape Lookout Light Vessel had reported that an unknown ship had passed the light vessel immediately after the *Deering* on January 29, and had seemed to be following the *Deering*. When the engineer tried to summon the ship to stop, it suspiciously sped up, dropping a tarp over its nameplate as it moved past the light vessel.

Another line of reasoning, especially popular among the locals, was that the *Deering* simply encountered a storm and was grounded on Diamond Shoals in the night. The captain and crewmen, afraid for their lives, escaped in their lifeboats but went under in the rough seas. They were probably at the bottom of the sea. But still, there were so many odd facts and variables to the story, so many unanswered questions.

Then, on April 10, 1921, a Hatteras native, Christopher Columbus Gray, was walking on the beach in Buxton and found a bottle containing a message. The note read as follows:

Deering Captured by Oil Burning Boat
Something Like Chaser taking Off everything
Handcuffing Crew
Crew hiding All over Ship no Chance to
Make escape finder please
notify head Qts of Deering

The investigation heated up. Handwriting experts compared the letter with other documents and claimed it was written by the *Deering's* engineer Herbert Bates. Secretary of Commerce Herbert Hoover got involved in the investigation, putting the best FBI agents on the trail. Newspapers followed the story regularly. There was a lot of speculation about what happened, but there wasn't enough hard evidence, even with the letter, to prove anything.

In the end, it turned out that Christopher Columbus Gray's letter was a fraud. Several months later, in August of 1921, federal investigator Lawrence Richey got him to confess that he had written the note himself. He did it to get attention in the ranks of the federal government, in hopes that his application to work at the Cape Hatteras Lighthouse might go through. Government jobs at the Coast Guard station, Weather Bureau, and lighthouse were good to have on the Outer Banks: There was little else to do for a living but fish.

No one ever figured out what happened to the crew of the *Carroll A. Deering*. It remains a mystery to this day. Her bow, capstan, and skeletal frame lay on the beach at Ocracoke for a long time, something the tourists loved to see. Then in September 1955, Hurricane Ione uprooted what was left of the *Deering* and washed her back to the beach on Hatteras Island. Wheeler Balance hauled the capstan and some timbers back to his service station and put them on display for the tourists. That's all that's left of the *Carroll A. Deering*.

Bombs Away
· 1923 ·

It was Wednesday, September 5, and Brig. Gen. Billy Mitchell was proving his point. One by one, the heavy DeHavilland DH4s and small Martin MB2 bombers raced down the sandy airstrip and climbed sharply toward the clouds. At the heavy roar of the engines, the residents of Hatteras Village stopped what they were doing and looked skyward.

They knew that the crates of bombs that had been sitting on the beach for weeks had been loaded into these planes. They knew the servicemen who had been stationed in their village since early August were finally conducting the task they had come to complete. They knew all about this mission because many of them had collected many a silver dollar to help Billy Mitchell build the crude airstrip on the oceanfront next to Durant's Coast Guard Station so that the military airplanes could take off and land in their village.

One by one the planes took off from the beach and headed north toward Cape Hatteras. On land, the villagers' reactions varied. Even though Mitchell had assured them they were in no danger, some of the islanders were afraid and ran for shelter, believing the bombs would drop from the planes too soon. Some villagers were so worried about the unforeseen outcomes of Mitchell's maneuvers that they fled from the village the day before. As the planes headed out of sight, other villagers went home to gather their good clothes and to prepare food for the celebration that was to come.

Meanwhile, 6 miles off Cape Hatteras, the pilots spotted their targets—two decommissioned battleships, the *New Jersey* and the *Virginia*. A ship full of members of the media and military onlookers, floating at a safe distance onboard the *St. Mihiel,* spotted the planes coming into sight.

Brigadier General Mitchell circled in his plane, surveying the activity of his airmen. They dropped the first bombs, although they missed their targets. Then, a second round dropped and contact was made. The airmen spent the better part of the day in the skies, bombing the ships from 10,000 feet in the air, then returning to the Hatteras Village "airdrome" to receive Mitchell's instructions and to gather supplies.

In the end, the battleship carcasses were under water, the fifth and sixth ships ever bombed by airplanes and the only ships in the Graveyard of the Atlantic sunk by friendly fire. Back at Langley Field in Virginia that night, Mitchell wrote the following in his journal:

> Spent practically the entire day in the air watching the bombardment of seacraft. After each flight I returned to the airdrome and issued instructions. The tests were completed successfully but many defects in our bombardment became manifest. The personnel situation is also becoming very acute and I doubt if we will be able to stage another demonstration of this nature unless we have a complete reorganization. Returned to Langley Field by air, arriving at the field just before dark.

Yes, Billy Mitchell had proven his point. For the second time, he had shown that airplanes could indeed sink battleships. Maybe now the nation's military leaders and politicians would heed his warnings that, with advances in modern aviation, battleships were not the only means of warfare. Maybe now they would establish the separate military air service he had been demanding.

Mitchell had done similar test bombings before. Two years earlier, in 1921, he had assembled the necessary military aircraft, bombs, and ships to conduct a series of bombing trials off the coast of Virginia. His trained airmen sank three captured German warships, including a battleship that had been deemed unsinkable, as well as an obsolete U.S. battleship.

The trials were part of Mitchell's quest to convince the military and the nation that "air power, both from a military and an economic standpoint, will not only dominate the land but the sea as well." Mitchell, an aviation military hero in World War I, was convinced that in future wars air power could defend the nation's coasts from attacks better than sea power. At that point in time, however, the notion was audacious.

It would seem that the first test would have settled the national debate as to whether an airplane could sink a battleship. But Mitchell's detractors and military superiors were not wholly convinced. They called the tests beginner's luck. Thus, two years later in North Carolina, within stricter guidelines imposed by the military, Mitchell completed his tests again. He proved that the military could protect the nation's coast by setting up small stations of airmen at places like Hatteras Village. With the right supplies and only a handmade airstrip for their planes, they could halt approaching enemy ships.

With the battleships at the bottom of the sea near Diamond Shoals, Mitchell and his airmen returned to the airdrome at Hatteras Village, where the local residents, wearing their Sunday best, were waiting to greet them. The locals might have been a far cry from the national press and big-wigs that had been waiting after the tests in Virginia, but the Hatteras residents were a welcome sight. They feted the airmen with a feast by the sea. Photographs were snapped, not for the nation's papers but for Hatteras family scrapbooks.

Hatteras Island in the early 1920s, remote and sparsely populated, was the last place one would expect to find a worldly military hero carrying out controversial war-tactics tests. However, Mitchell had been to Hatteras Village many times before. An avid outdoorsman, he first visited the island because of its well-known reputation for waterfowl shooting. Stationed in Virginia following World War I, Mitchell often traveled south to Hatteras in his leisure time.

Always wearing knee-high cavalry boots around the village, Mitchell was a frequent visitor in the community. He dined with a local family, stood in duck blinds on Pamlico Sound, and fished out of Hatteras Inlet. One memorable photograph shows him on the porch of a Hatteras cottage with a bag of ducks, while another shows him on the docks next to a huge yellow-fin tuna. Aviation made it easy for Mitchell to make a quick escape to Hatteras, landing his DeHavilland on the hardest patch of sand he could find. Though it was nearly two decades after the Wright brothers' first flight, Mitchell's plane was probably the first airplane many of the Hatteras Islanders had ever seen. After numerous trips to Hatteras only for leisure, Mitchell began to see the possibilities for combining business and pleasure. The island seemed the perfect place to prove his theories about using air power to protect the nation's coast from approaching military ships. It's said that Mitchell had originally wanted his 1921 tests to be conducted off of Hatteras Island but the location had been changed to Virginia. When it came to his second round of tests, the Hatteras location came through.

Mitchell hired the locals to build the airstrip then sent a crew of about 30 men to live and train there. When the airmen arrived at their camp next to Durant's Coast Guard Station, the local surfmen had a good laugh at the airmen's attempts to set up tents in the wind and to keep the mosquitoes away. Eventually the surfmen invited the airmen into their station and the two groups cohabitated peacefully for the next several weeks. Today, the airstrip location is underwater.

Mitchell rarely visited Hatteras in the years that followed his 1923 bombing tests. The national air power debate got hot and he was often in Washington testifying to Congress. Mitchell became so outspoken and controversial, often criticizing his superiors in the press, that he was demoted to colonel and transferred to Texas. In 1925 he was court-martialed for insubordination, and in 1926 he resigned from military service.

Like many iconic personalities, Mitchell was either deeply admired or fiercely detested. Politicians and military leaders loathed his arrogance and outspokenness, whereas supporters of air power and many civilians loved his undiplomatic ways. The people of Hatteras loved Billy Mitchell. It's said that the famous general was soft-spoken and inquisitive among them. Despite his contentious reputation, the villagers remember only the good things about the man who liked it so much on their island. They thought so much of the general that his name still lingers on the island today, on a road sign, a motel's name, and in the National Park Service's Billy Mitchell Airstrip in Frisco.

The Park That Almost Wasn't

· 1933 ·

The article in the July 21, 1933, Elizabeth City *Independent* was like a beacon of hope to the people of the Outer Banks. "A Coastal Park for North Carolina and the Nation" ran the headline. The accompanying story, written by Outer Banks resident Frank Stick, proposed that North Carolina's barrier islands, which ran from the Virginia border all the way through the middle of the state at Cape Lookout, should be established as a national park. Stick's idea was to acquire the barren lands between the widely scattered Outer Banks villages and preserve them as parklands for recreation, wildlife conservation, and the protection of the coastline in the event of war. Stick's vision for the park also included Fort Raleigh on Roanoke Island, site of the first attempted English colony in the New World, and Kill Devil Hill, where the Wright brothers flew the first airplane. According to Stick's proposal, the park's focal point would be Cape Hatteras. Some of the land would be kept in its natural state, some would be made accessible for recreation. Bridges would be built to cross the inlets. Roads would be paved to access the park. Best of all, Stick wrote, it would bring much-needed vitalization to the Outer Banks, in the form of tourism.

Tourism meant revenue. Tourism meant employment. Tourism meant a way out of the Depression-era slump the

Outer Banks was in. It was only an idea, a proposal in the local newspaper, but to the people of the Outer Banks it was the only chance for change. Nearly all of the five thousand residents from Corolla to Roanoke Island to Ocracoke were in favor of Stick's idea.

The Bankers were struggling, not just because of the Great Depression but because of many other factors as well. The old ways of making a living were not as prosperous as they had been, not that anyone had ever made a fortune on the isolated Outer Banks. Stricter hunting laws and a shortage of waterfowl meant no more commercial hunting and fewer jobs at the gun clubs established by wealthy Northerners as hunting retreats. Maritime traffic no longer used the Outer Banks inlets in a significant way. The livestock were weak, the fishing was slow, and there was no market for porpoise or yaupon, which had once been Outer Banks commodities. The only steady jobs were at one of four lighthouses or with the U.S. Coast Guard at the lifesaving stations. And with shipwrecks becoming less common, there was a decreased need for lifesavers. As for tourism, it was extremely rare, except in Nags Head. There were no roads or bridges to connect the far-flung villages on Hatteras Island, Ocracoke Island, or the northernmost Outer Banks.

Even more problematic were hurricanes and flooding. At that time the Outer Banks was a flat expanse of sand from sea to sound, an issue that was exacerbated by free-roaming livestock eating all the shrubs and grasses, as well as the fact that the human inhabitants had cut down nearly all the trees for shipbuilding. Every time a hurricane or major storm hit the Outer Banks, water would wash clean over the islands, from sea to sound or sound to sea, ravaging structures, gardens, and livelihoods. Villages were dying out. People were moving away. Those who stayed constantly battled the elements.

Stick's article, and several others that followed, revealed a rehabilitation plan for the Outer Banks. A nationally known artist as well as a real estate developer, Stick was one of few men who foresaw the future value of the Outer Banks lands. Stick admitted that first the erosion problem would have to be addressed. After the land was stabilized, he said, the park would be more feasible and access roads and bridges could be built.

In August and September of 1933 two powerful hurricanes hit the Outer Banks. The villages flooded, and New Inlet re-opened on Hatteras Island's northern end, blocking access to the island's villages from the north. People were devastated. Something had to be done.

In response to the park proposal and erosion problems, the North Carolina Coastal Development Commission was es-tablished. In September 1933 Stick and the commission arranged a tour for newspaper reporters and top state decision-makers, most of whom had never seen the Outer Banks. The tour included New Inlet and Pea Island by a local lifesaving hero, a seafood feast in the village of Kinnakeet, a visit to the Kinnakeet Gun Club, a beach ride out to Cape Point, and a trip through Buxton Woods. Every one of the visitors was in awe of the beauty they saw and the hospitality they received on Hat-teras Island. The officials saw the need for erosion control, and the reporters spread the park idea far and wide. Things were looking favorable for the national seashore park.

The North Carolina Coastal Development Commission called for an erosion control plan, or a "sand-fixation project," to protect the Outer Banks from further erosion and storm dam-age. They proposed building barrier dunes along the ocean-front, thereby re-establishing vegetation and putting people to work in the process. It just so happened that they had all the manpower they needed to get such a job done: Roosevelt's New Deal was looking for ways to employ the nation's men. On November 21, 1933, the federal Civil Works Administration promised funds of more than a million dollars for the project.

From 1935 through 1940 the Civilian Conservation Corps (CCC) and Works Progress Administration (WPA) set up camps along the Outer Banks and built 150 miles of massive ocean-front dunes from Corolla through Ocracoke. They erected sand fences and piled brush to collect blowing sand, then planted stabilizing grasses on the dunes to keep them in place. They used over 600 miles of sand-fencing and planted more than a million square feet of grasses and more than two million trees and shrubs. Their work dramatically changed the Outer Banks. The oceanfront dunes they built still stand today.

In 1937, North Carolina Representative Lindsay Warren introduced a bill to Congress requesting the creation of the Cape Hatteras National Seashore. Congress approved the bill, effectively creating the first such park in the nation, the first national seashore. The park had no land holdings, so the Cape Hatteras National Seashore Commission began seeking land donations, which were held in trust by the state until they were all collected. The first major donation was of 1,200 acres spread out between Kinnakeet and Hatteras Inlet, which was donated by the Phipps family.

Everything was working in favor of the park until World War II started. As the nation's attention turned elsewhere, land acquisition for the park ceased. There were much more important things to worry about until the war was over.

But when World War II ended, the Cape Hatteras National Seashore project was not revived. Hatteras and Ocracoke residents were now very much opposed to the park, thanks to Standard Oil Company, which came to Hatteras Island during the war, buying up mineral rights and test drilling for oil. The prospect of getting rich off oil was much more alluring than handing over land to the government.

Also contributing to the park's demise was the fact that tourism picked up in Nags Head, Kill Devil Hills, and Kitty Hawk after the war. The residents there didn't want to cut off their prospects for growth, and thus the community business leaders bitterly opposed the park.

In 1945 Congress passed a bill calling for the indefinite postponement of the park. In 1947 the state terminated its involvement in the project and authorized the return of all properties to their owners.

The project was dead. Cape Hatteras National Seashore was not to be.

In late 1948 David Stick, Frank's son, moved back to Dare County and learned what had happened to his father's dream. He called his father, who had moved away, and the two contacted friends in the National Park Service and state government. They learned that the park service, as well as many North Carolina leaders, still supported the project. The Sticks learned that while there was still time to revive the project, there was also extreme local opposition to its establishment, even though Standard Oil Company had found not one drop of oil on the Outer Banks.

At the behest of Rep. Dewey Hayman, the North Carolina General Assembly passed a bill reactivating the Cape Hatteras National Seashore Commission. The National Park Service expressed its plans to go ahead with the project.

The locals were outraged. But promises were made in an attempt to turn their minds around. The park's scope shrank to just Hatteras and Ocracoke islands. The National Park Service promised the locals the park would not include the established villages, that it would still offer hunting, fishing, and beach access, and that a road would be built the length of Hatteras Island.

In June 1952 came a boon for the park. Two Mellon family foundations offered to give nearly $620,000 for the purchase of parklands if the state would agree to match its funds. The state agreed. The locals came around slowly, and in the end many agreed to sell their land. Local families were paid between $5 and $75 an acre for their barrier island land, which today, descendants of those landowners say, was not at all a fair price.

On December 22, 1952, nineteen years after the initial suggestion for the park, twenty-eight thousand acres on Hatteras and Ocracoke islands were turned over to the National Park Service. Nearly 85 percent of the islands was preserved as the nation's first national seashore. On January 17, 1953, Cape Hatteras National Seashore was officially established.

Though many families on Hatteras and Ocracoke islands feel like they were paid too little for the land and many of the locals butt heads with the Park Service, most everyone agrees that the preservation of the Cape Hatteras National Seashore is what makes the Outer Banks so special. Eighty-five percent of the islands is preserved in its natural state. Frank Stick's vision of revitalization became reality: More than 3.5 million people visit the seashore every year, and tourism is by far the dominant industry on Hatteras and Ocracoke Islands.

Terror in Torpedo Junction

· 1942 ·

It was just after 2:00 A.M. on January 18, 1942. Below deck, the crewmen were sleeping, playing cards, or tending to the routine duties of transporting fuel up the eastern seaboard. Second Mate Melvin Rand, on late duty, peered groggily from the bridge of the oil tanker, *Allan Jackson,* into the dark, endless ocean around him. Beside him, Seaman Randy Larson had the wheel. Bound for New York with more than 72,000 barrels of crude oil, the ship was traveling 75 miles from shore, giving Cape Hatteras a wide berth.

Rand's eye caught an odd sight to starboard, a spontaneous wake moving toward the ship. Rand's first thought was that it looked like a torpedo, but it couldn't be. Could it? "Hard to port!" he shouted to Larson.

A deafening explosion blasted the ship as the torpedo smacked into the bow. Another explosion ransacked the starboard side, and the *Allan Jackson* burst into flames. Rand and Larson jumped into the freezing winter sea. Captain Felix W. Kretchmer, tossed from his bunk by the second explosion, escaped his fiery cabin by squeezing through a porthole, but as soon as he was free the ship split in two and he was washed into the sea. Oil oozed from the ship, and flames engulfed the water, extending as much as a half-mile outward. Burning men leapt from the ship into the sea. Several seamen made it to a lifeboat, rowing as fast as they could from the carnage.

German Commander Richard Zapp, at a comfortable distance on board the *U-66*, surveyed the damage. This was what he had come to Cape Hatteras to do. At his orders, the *U-66* eased under the ocean's surface and slipped away from the scene unnoticed.

Hours later, an American destroyer, the *Roe*, was on a routine patrol and came upon the fiery scene. The *Roe* crew rescued the *Allan Jackson* survivors, including Rand and Larson and the men in the lifeboat. They looked in horror at the burned bodies floating in the sea. Twenty-two men were dead. Before heading off to Norfolk, a crewman on the *Roe* observed that one of the floating bodies was moving in the water. Captain Kretchmer was pulled out of the sea alive seven hours after the attack.

The next night, January 19, Zapp's next target was a Canadian passenger liner, the *Lady Hawkins*, moving past Cape Hatteras. The *U-66* torpedoed it twice, spilling three hundred passengers and crew into the icy water. Only ninety-six people survived.

Meanwhile, another German commander was moving his U-boat to the Outer Banks. The same night that Zapp shot down the *Lady Hawkins*, Captain Reinhard Hardegen, onboard the *U-123*, torpedoed the *City of Atlanta* seven miles east of Avon, North Carolina, killing forty-four of forty-seven men on board. About three hours later, the *U-123* hit again, this time the *Ciltvaira*, a small Latvian freighter whose crew escaped in a lifeboat. Less than two hours later he struck another tanker, the *Malay*, near Diamond Shoals, this time with guns instead of a torpedo. The *Malay*, which happened to be empty of cargo, was badly damaged but managed to make it to Norfolk without sinking.

The *U-123* left Cape Hatteras to head back to its port in France, but the *U-66* stayed around Hatteras for a few more days, knocking off three more Allied vessels traveling on the shipping lanes around the Outer Banks before also returning to port in France. Soon two new boats, the *U-125* and the *U-130*, would arrive at Cape Hatteras.

To the merchant seamen and crewmen whose job it was to transport tankers and freighters past Cape Hatteras, the infamous weather and shoals of the Graveyard of the Atlantic now seemed a minor concern. A new threat, in the form of the Germans and their sly U-boats, was much more fearsome, earning the Graveyard of the Atlantic a new nickname: "Torpedo Junction."

The German attack in January of 1942 was part of *Paukenschlag*, which loosely translated into "Operation Drumroll" (although it was sometimes called "Drumbeat"), a mission started on January 13, 1942, at the beginning of World War II. Led by German Admiral Karl Doenitz, the mission was a planned attack on American and British shipping all along the East Coast. Their plan was to destroy as much tonnage as possible, in essence cutting the supply lines of the United States and Britain. The Germans were successful beyond belief.

The German U-boats were submersible ships, which could descend at will to evade an enemy, to attack, or to avoid stormy weather. The boats normally traveled above water and had enough fuel to leave France, reach the coast of America, and hunt the enemy for about a week before returning to France. During the first six months of 1942, German U-boats torpedoed 397 ships along the eastern seaboard of the United States, from New England to the Caribbean to the Gulf of Mexico. Nearly five thousand people died in these attacks. "The largest concentration of losses took place in the waters off North Carolina's Outer Banks, an area notorious for centuries as a graveyard of ships," wrote Kevin Duffus in his documentary film about Torpedo Junction, *War Zone: Infamy, Irony and Innocence Lost on the Outer Banks in 1942.*

The people on the Outer Banks in 1942 were very aware of what was going on around them. Many natives remember the sights and sounds of war being waged in their own back-yard, especially on Hatteras and Ocracoke islands, but also as far north as Corolla. The Bankers experienced window-rattling explosions, saw the fires burning at sea, and found oil, debris, and bodies washing onto their shores. "There would be great explosions, even in the middle of day," said Carol Dillon, who grew up in Buxton. "The windows of the schoolhouse would shake like they were going to explode too." In Ocracoke, Blanche Joliff heard the explosions too. "It would shake the houses and sometimes the explosions cracked the cistern and damaged the sheet rock and plaster in some of the houses," she told Kevin Duffus for the documentary *War Zone.*

The month of March was extremely deadly off the Outer Banks. One U-boat sank nine ships in seven days, and there were other attacks as well. The ocean was black with oil spilled from bombed freighters. Some Outer Banks families had buck-ets of water on their porches to wash the oil from their feet when they came in from the beach. The radio waves were jammed with calls of ships in trouble. The Coast Guard stations on the Outer Banks were overwhelmed with washed-up sur-vivors. One local man, Aycock Brown, who worked as a civil-ian agent for U.S. Naval Intelligence, was extremely busy identifying all the dead bodies that washed ashore on the Outer Banks or that were recovered at sea.

To the Germans' surprise, the United States didn't put up much resistance in the beginning. Furthermore, no one made any effort to darken the lights along the coast, which made it very easy for the Germans to navigate as well as to see their targets. The tankers and freighters they were looking for formed perfect silhouettes against the backdrop of lights in the coastal towns. Finally, after two months of attacks, the Navy caught on, ordering the coastal towns darkened at night. Outer Banks residents stretched black tape over their headlights and blackened their windows with heavy drapes. There was to be no driving on the beach at night. The Navy also began to form convoys of merchant ships and allowed merchant ships to travel only in the daytime.

The East Coast was barely guarded at all. Sixty-five German U-boats hunted Allied merchant vessels practically unopposed. It would be two months before the U.S. Navy successfully retaliated against the German U-boats.

The first sinking of a German U-boat by an American ship didn't occur until April 13, 1942. It happened off Wimble Shoals, near Nags Head, when the USS *Jesse Roper,* a Navy destroyer, spotted a mysterious ship nearby. The *Roper* chased the ship down and caught up with it, realizing it was a German U-boat as it approached. The ship, the *U-85,* defensively sent a torpedo toward the *Roper,* but it just missed the American ship. Navy crewmen aboard the *Jesse Roper* then fired a machine gun toward the U-85, killing numerous German gunmen who had been ordered onto the deck. Amidst a barrage of U.S. gunfire, the U-boat began to sink. The *Roper* sent a series of underwater depth charges to the spot of the sinking ship, and a mass of air bubbles and oil slicks indicated she was gone. The Americans, when they were sure the U-boat was gone and there were no others in the area, later recovered twenty-nine bodies from the sea, which they took to Norfolk and gave a proper burial.

The Americans shot down only six more U-boats after the *U-85,* resulting in the deaths of approximately 300 Germans. It was hardly a show compared to the 5,000 Allied seamen and 397 Allied ships the Germans had downed. More than five dozen ships, victims of the German U-boats, lie on the ocean floor off North Carolina today, most of them off the Outer Banks.

The Fish That Started It All

· 1951 ·

In the summer of 1951, Captain Ernal Foster of Hatteras Village was determined to catch a blue marlin. As owner of the *Albatross I* and *II*, the first recreational charter fishing boats on the Outer Banks, he spent a great deal of time in the Gulf Stream and had hooked many of the prized fish. But he could never seem to bring a blue marlin all the way into the boat. The big, blue beast of the sea had eluded him thus far, but he was determined to change that.

One summer day, on the water with a fishing party, Foster saw a blue marlin go after a feather tied to one of his 6-0 fishing rigs. But Foster reeled in the lure before the fish could bite, knowing that if he tried to catch the fish on a rig that small he would lose his line and lure, as he had many times before. The next time a blue marlin came around, he would be ready.

That night, Foster rigged a 9-0 Penn Senator reel with 70-pound test linen line, just in case a big blue showed up at the next day's fishing charter in the Gulf Stream. This was the same rig that some recreational anglers had told him they used to catch blue marlin in Florida waters. Blue marlin, a trophy fish prized for its size and incredible ability to fight, were caught in abundance in the Caribbean and Florida, and their presence was well known around Hatteras. Blue marlin had been caught in Hatteras waters before, starting with New Jersey angler Hugh

Rutherford on a private yacht in 1939. But no one had caught a blue marlin off Hatteras since recreational fishing resumed in the village after World War II, and no local man had ever snagged one of the fish. As operator of the only recreational fishing fleet on the Outer Banks, Foster knew his catch was overdue.

The next day, the *Albatross II* motored around offshore with a fishing party of gentlemen who were interested in going after sailfish and small game fish. Foster's brother Gaston was operating the boat, while Foster served as mate, helping get bait into the water and assisting with the landing of fish.

About the middle of the day, when the anglers paused for lunch, Ernal spotted what he had hoped for—a blue marlin. He free-spooled some mackerel chunks out to the marlin on his new 9-0 rig. The fish gladly took the bait, and Ernal jerked the hook.

"Does anyone want to catch a big fish?" he asked, offering the rod and reel to the members of the fishing party. They all declined. The big fish was not jumping out of the water, and the novice anglers were afraid it was a shark. They pled with Foster to cut the line, to let the fish go. But he had no intention of doing that.

With no harness or belt to help him anchor the rod butt, Foster fought the fish, reeling as hard as he could. Gaston watched from the wheel, helping position the boat for an easier fight. The fishing party watched in awe as the captain battled a sea beast more than twice his size. The struggle went on for well over two hours.

At long last, Foster defeated the fish. The blue marlin died with the hook still in its mouth, but it died down deep. The end of the battle required Foster to haul the dead weight of the fish up to the surface with his already-exhausted reeling arm. All the men on board helped haul the beautiful blue marlin into the stern of the *Albatross II*, and they headed back to Foster's Quay in Hatteras harbor.

Back at the Hatteras docks, a crowd of locals and anglers gathered around the *Albatross II* to see the fish. A rope was tied around the fish's tail and it was yanked onto the scales. It weighed in at four hundred and seventy-five pounds. Dare County's ever-present publicist, Aycock Brown, was at the docks and snapped a photo of the blue marlin. The photo and story were sent to newspapers all along the East Coast, and the word was out about blue marlin fishing out of Hatteras Inlet.

Looking back years later, Ernal Foster saw that fish as one of the turning points in Hatteras sport fishing. Today, on the bulletin board in the office at Foster's Quay, among a collage of black and white fishing photos, the photograph of that marlin hanging on the scales is captioned THE FISH THAT STARTED IT ALL.

Another blue marlin caught on the *Albatross II* also captured a lot of attention because it was the first blue marlin caught north of Florida by a woman. Mr. and Mrs. Ross Walker of Richmond, Virginia, frequently fished with Foster, and in 1952 it was Mrs. Walker who reeled in a big blue. It took hours to get the marlin to the boat, but when the *Albatross II* finally pulled into the docks after dark, a crowd was waiting to congratulate Mrs. Walker.

By 1953, catching blue marlin around Hatteras was commonplace, and fishing was so good and so widely reported that Foster had to build a third boat, the *Albatross III,* to take all the anglers who wanted to go. A second charter captain also started running recreational trips out of Hatteras. Up to that point, Foster had been the only captain on the entire Outer Banks whose charters were dedicated to recreational fishing. Other fishermen combined commercial and recreational fishing, but Foster had committed to recreational fishing with foresight in the late 1930s. In the early years he'd had to motor 25 miles across the sound to pick up his customers in Engelhard, but as the word spread about fishing off Hatteras, more and more anglers were coming to him.

Fishing for blue marlin out of Hatteras definitely had its advantages, especially geographically. On the banks of deep Hatteras Inlet and less than 20 miles from the Gulf Stream, Hatteras Village is perfectly positioned for offshore fishing. It offers the closest access to the Gulf Stream north of Florida. And in the days before GPS and radar, boat captains around Hatteras could always get their bearings by looking for the Cape Hatteras Lighthouse or the Diamond Shoals Lightship, a ship that sat anchored on Diamond Shoals to warn approaching boats of the navigational hazard. Anglers in other areas didn't have such easy markers.

In August 1958, yet another notable and unusual event happened on board the *Albatross II*. Jack and Ellie Cleveland of Greenwich, Connecticut, chartered Foster's boat for the day to fish for blue marlin. Jack Cleveland caught a blue marlin that day, but instead of bringing it back to the docks, Cleveland insisted that his marlin be released back to the sea. It was the first deliberate release of a blue marlin, and people in the village were flabbergasted at this act of conservation. The common practice in that day was to bring the trophy fish back to the docks to show it off, as well as to rot, as there was no use for the fish.

"People thought they were crazy," said Ernie Foster, son of Ernal Foster. "There was a lot of ridicule and snide comments." The Clevelands' deed didn't change fishing practices for a long time to come, but it got people talking all along the East Coast.

Blue marlin fishing was so good around Hatteras that big-time anglers began frequenting the tiny island village in their private yachts. Several of them got together and formed the Hatteras Marlin Club, and in 1959 they started the Hatteras Marlin Club International Blue Marlin Tournament. The tournaments were a huge success. Lloyd Styron, who was the tournament's weigh master for twelve years, said, "Several times we had so many fish hanging on the rack that we had to lay them on the ground. We were afraid the rack would collapse."

The day before the 1962 tournament was set to begin, the *Albatross II* again created another blue marlin stir. On June 11, 1962, Gary Stokes, an angler on board the *Albatross II,* caught the biggest blue marlin anyone on the boat had ever seen. Captain Bill Foster certainly had never seen one so big. The fish jumped completely from the water fifteen times in twenty minutes before yielding to the angler and dying at the side of the boat as it was gaffed by the mate. The anglers proudly brought the big blue back to the docks.

When Stokes's blue marlin was pulled on to the scales, it weighed 810 pounds. It was the largest blue marlin ever caught on rod and reel and the largest ever caught on artificial bait, setting a new world record.

The timing couldn't have been better. The world-record fish hung on the scales before the eyes of all the people in town for the tournament—international anglers, outdoor writers, charter parties, and private yachtsmen alike. A sports reporter for *The Virginian-Pilot* wrote in the next day's paper, "Let no man now dispute Hatteras' claim to the title 'Blue Marlin Capital of the World.' The proof is now a matter of record."

Though the current record was broken in 1974 by an angler who caught a 1,142-pound blue marlin elsewhere, Hatteras Village still goes by that moniker in many circles.

Today there are seven marinas and nearly thirty-five charter boats fishing out of Hatteras harbor. The annual Blue Marlin Tournament, still going strong, celebrated its forty-fifth year in 2004. Now, however, it's a catch-and-release tournament. Many people credit the Foster family and the *Albatross* fleet—as well as Ernal Foster's first blue marlin catch—for helping establish Hatteras Village as the "Blue Marlin Capital of the World."

The Big Night
• 1958 •

Promotional posters were tacked to nearly every telephone pole in Dare and Currituck Counties. Ads in *The Coastland Times* promoted the "biggest night of entertainment at Nags Head in years." The word passed from the mouths of music lovers all the way from Nags Head to Hatteras Island to Little Washington to Virginia Beach: Louis Armstrong and his band were coming to The Casino.

This was not the first big-name band to play at the venerable Nags Head institution. Since George "Ras" Wescott had bought the dance hall/bowling alley in 1937, crowds had gotten used to seeing some of the greatest names in music come to out-of-the-way Nags Head. Duke Ellington, Tommy Dorsey, Glenn Miller, Artie Shaw, Fats Domino, Jerry Lee Lewis, the Inkspots, and many others traveled to Nags Head to play the legendary Casino, which was curiously named since there wasn't a gambling outlet in sight. But even among those big names, "Satchmo," as Armstrong was known, was one of the greatest acts in jazz, and there was bound to be an all-time record crowd.

Thirty-one-year-old Roanoke Island native Woodie Fearing wasn't going to miss this show for anything. A jazz fanatic, he'd wanted to see Louis Armstrong since he was a student at UNC-Chapel Hill in the early 1950s. As a member of the selection committee for bringing bands to campus, Fearing had repeatedly voted for Armstrong. But the very weekend that Satchmo finally played on campus in 1954, Fearing was called home to Roanoke Island for a family matter.

So on Saturday, July 12, 1958, Fearing made sure he was at The Casino early. The evening was still hot and humid as he drove along the Beach Road to the great dance club. The club was a former barracks house for the stone masons that built the Wright Brothers National Memorial and it backed right up to Nags Head's landmark sand dune, Jockey's Ridge. Jukebox music spilled out of the windows, which were propped open to catch the sea breezes and cool the un-air-conditioned building.

Miss Delnoy Burrus, at the ticket booth with her little dog Beauty, greeted Fearing and took his money for two five-dollar tickets, one for him and one for his wife, Betty. Downstairs the kids were bowling and eating hot dogs, just as Fearing had done when he was a teenager. He'd first been to The Casino as a boy of twelve, delivering bread and hot dog rolls for his family's Wonder Bread franchise, and the dance club had been a part of his life ever since. He'd taken dates there in high school and danced barefoot on the floor polished slick with bowling alley wax. Going barefoot was the rule at The Casino. He'd gone there with his fellow guardsmen when he was working at the Nags Head Coast Guard station, dancing barefoot even when he was in uniform. He'd seen countless bands in the up-stairs dance hall, but to him this night was more special than them all.

At the top of the stairs, the Fearings and everyone else ditched their shoes. Even though it was early, a crowd was gathering, claiming their tables around the perimeter of the dance floor and ordering Pabst Blue Ribbon at the bar.

Often called the "Barefoot Bar," The Casino regularly drew fun-lovers from hundreds of miles away. People didn't mind driving an hour or two from Edenton or Norfolk or farther, es-pecially on a summer weekend. The Casino was always worth it. Four years earlier Fats Domino had played there, winning the local crowd over when he sang "I found my thrill on Jockey's Ridge," though it didn't have nearly the ring of the original. It's said as many as 1,500 people packed into the building that night, standing on the tables and dancing nose to nose.

As the sun sunk lower behind Jockey's Ridge, Armstrong's band was setting up for its 9:00 P.M. show. There was no backstage area at The Casino where the performers could prepare or wait, so it wasn't long before Fearing spotted Velma Middleton, Armstrong's singer, sitting alone at a table near the stage. "I went up and introduced myself," Fearing remembers. "I told her I'd waited eight years to see her. She said she was pleased to know I'd waited that long."

With show time nearing, Fearing worked his way through the crowd, which was thick, with at least as many fans as at the Fats Domino show, and maybe more. At 9:00, with the temperature rising from all those bodies crammed on the dance floor, the band came on. There was Armstrong on trumpet, Middleton as vocalist, Trummy Young on trombone, Barrett Deems on drums, Edmond Hall on clarinet, Billy Kyle on piano, Arvell Shaw on bass, and Woodie Fearing on front row.

With the first burst of music, it became apparent that the mike stand was broken. Middleton and Armstrong were sharing the microphone, but the microphone stand wouldn't stay extended. The microphone slipped down every time Middleton lifted it back up. On instinct, Fearing reached out and held the stand so the mike would stay up. He stayed that way, arm outstretched, practically on stage with the band, for the rest of the night. His wife went off to dance, but Fearing stayed where he was, incredulous of his great fortune. "I missed the dancing, but I had the music ringing in my ears," Fearing later said.

Meanwhile, another die-hard jazz fan from Roanoke Island didn't share in Fearing's luck but still found a way to enjoy the show. Lebame Houston was too young to get into the show, and her mother wouldn't have let her go anyway. She also had to dance in the local production of *The Lost Colony* that night, but still she found a way to hear Louis Armstrong. Houston, who was an Indian dancer in the play, performed the opening dance in the show, then faked a sprained ankle and high-tailed it over the bridge to Nags Head. She couldn't get upstairs to see the band, so she hung out by an open window next to the ticket booth and soaked up every note.

Unlike Houston, Fearing saw everything—Middleton swaying as she sang in her saucy voice, Armstrong working himself into a sweat and wiping his dripping brow with a handkerchief, the spit shaking out of his trumpet. Fearing knew every song, singing along and dancing the best he could while holding the microphone. He left his spot only once during the three-hour show, getting someone else to hold the mike so he could dance a song with his wife.

"It was a great show," said Fearing. "Even though I was anchored, I enjoyed every minute of it. If I had to do it all over again, I'd do it just the same way," he proudly told a newspaper reporter in 2000. At one point, during a break, Fearing tried to speak to Armstrong. But the crowd was so loud that Armstrong couldn't hear him. He repeated himself several times to no avail.

Some reports said there were 2,000 people in The Casino that night. It was one of the biggest nights The Casino ever had, but it certainly wasn't the last. The Casino continued to thrive in Nags Head throughout the 1960s, though at that time the music changed from 1950s rock 'n roll, just as it had done when the 1940s swing went out of fashion.

In the 1960s, beach music took over. Bill Deal and the Rhondells, Maurice Williams and the Zodiacs, the Drifters, and the Hot Nuts became the favorites, with the dancers doing a shuffling dance called the shag. Owner Ras Wescott may have had a little trouble with the changing times. He didn't want any of the 1960s long-haired men in his club, so he created a place on the dunes behind his club that he called "Monkey World," where he let the long hairs hang out. If a man with long hair really wanted to get in, Miss Delnoy kept a pair of scissors at the ticket booth to make him presentable enough for Wescott's eyes.

Wescott sold The Casino in the 1970s and the new owner called the club Nepethe. Such names as Blood, Sweat and Tears, John Prine, and the Four Tops played there in the 1970s, but the club never had the popularity of The Casino. The building was the same, but the soul of The Casino was already gone. In 1976, a nor'easter dumped so much rain on the building that the roof collapsed. The building was burned in 1981 as practice for the Nags Head Fire Department. In its place today is a sprawling shopping complex.

The Casino may be gone but it certainly lives on in the memories of longtime locals and visitors, those who jitterbugged in the 1940s, bopped in the 1950s, shagged in the 1960s, rocked in the 1970s, and especially in those that enjoyed Armstrong that big night in 1958.

Creating the Carolina Boat

· 1959 ·

One of the most memorable sights on the Outer Banks is the rainbow-colored fleet of locally made Carolina sport-fishing boats lining up for the daily return trip through Oregon Inlet in the late afternoon. Each brightly painted beauty is illuminated by the sinking sun. The hulls, which form a beautifully sharp V, cut through the water like knives through butter, the sensually arced, flared bows returning the spray to the sea.

Renowned for their seaworthiness, fishing prowess, and beauty, Carolina boats are seen all around the world today. But they will always be most at home in the waters of the Outer Banks, maneuvering through the notoriously choppy inlets, slicing through the headseas of a northeast blow, rocking gently on the swells of the Gulf Stream. These are the conditions the boats were created to handle. The Carolina boat is a product of the Outer Banks, a reflection of its sea conditions, its weather, and its people.

In the early days of charter fishing on the northern Outer Banks, in the 1950s, the local captains were commercial fishermen who spent their winters gathering fish and their summers toting tourists to the Gulf Stream. They required super-seaworthy boats so they could go offshore more often, even on those rough, windy days that the Outer Banks offers up regularly. And they needed their boats to run quickly and economically. Thus, the history and evolution of the Carolina boat is purely functional, designed to keep these fishermen in business.

One of the most distinctive features of the Carolina boat is its flared bow. The fishermen and boat builders of Harkers Island, south of the Outer Banks, first developed that trademark flare to keep the boat decks and the passengers dry. On Hatteras Island, captain and builder Ernal Foster was the first to exaggerate the flare for his Albatross fishing fleet.

But it's a Roanoke Island fisherman, Captain Warren O'Neal, who is widely considered the father of the benchmark Carolina boat hull. He was the first boat builder to combine the basic hull elements that are still being used by the Carolina boat builders today. He operated the first full-time boat shop on Roanoke Island, now the headquarters of Carolina boat building, and taught many of the great Outer Banks boat builders.

From humble beginnings in a small, waterfront boat shop, O'Neal left a legacy that evolved into an empire. Warren Robinson O'Neal was destined for a maritime life, born in 1909 to a family of "salts," including ship captains, fishermen, and light keepers, who had lived on the Outer Banks since his great-grandfather washed ashore at Salvo in a shipwreck. The family moved to Manteo and owned a sizable chunk of land along Dough's Creek, just off Shallowbag Bay.

Like many of Manteo's native sons, O'Neal and his brother developed a love for fishing and boats. While they were in high school, the boys built a backyard skiff, a 20-foot flat-bottom powered by a four-cylinder Model A Ford engine, and used it to fish their shad nets at Oregon Inlet.

After a year of college at Duke and a short stint in Chicago, O'Neal moved home to Roanoke Island to fish. He met and married a Wanchese girl, Pearl Daniels, and settled down in his family's Manteo home. He left the Outer Banks during World War II to work at a shipyard in Norfolk, but soon he was back on the Banks, working as a commercial fisherman for a living. In 1954 O'Neal bought a 40-foot, square-sterned boat and named it the

Pearl, after his wife. He commercial fished in the winter and ran fishing charters in the summer. When tourist season came around, he'd simply take out the *Pearl's* commercial rigging, add a fish-fighting chair, and start booking parties. O'Neal made a foray into boat construction with the refitting of the *Pearl,* but otherwise he was a fisherman.

Fate has a way of turning things around. Enter Omie Tillett, a young local fisherman and charter captain, who in 1959 approached O'Neal about building him a charter boat. While fishing in Florida, Tillett had admired the design of the sport-fishing boats built by John Rybovich & Sons in West Palm Beach. He brought photos of a Rybovich back to Roanoke Island and showed them to O'Neal in hopes of getting a similar boat. O'Neal was interested in the job, even though he had never built such a large boat. "I'd been around him, saw him working on his own boat and some others," says Tillett. "Plus he was interested and there weren't too many boat builders around here back then."

The two men made a trip to Norfolk to see a Rybovich because back then, unlike today, the world's fishing boats didn't come to the Outer Banks. Though he wasn't professionally trained as a draftsman, O'Neal sketched a boat design according to Tillett's wishes, borrowing the shearline, S-frame (the transition from the tumblehome to the flare), and cabin style from the Rybovich. To his design, O'Neal added a slightly sharper entry at the forefront of the hull.

O'Neal built a boat shop on his family's property on Dough's Creek in Manteo and, along with Tillett and a few other helpers, taught himself the art of boat building. They fished on good days and built the boat in the winter and on bad-weather days.

"There was no one around here to learn it from," O'Neal said in a 1997 interview. "I thought I could do it so I tried it."

The resulting 40-foot *Sportsman* was finished in 1960. It made an immediate and favorable impression on the local fishermen and set a precedent for boats to come. Soothing to the eye and stable at sea, it marked the beginning of a new style of boat building on the Outer Banks. "The S-frame had never been used here, but it was the going thing at Rybovich," says Tillett. "I told Warren what I liked and he put together a good boat. Of course, anytime you build you correct mistakes. The next one is always better." O'Neal, in an interview in 1997, remembered that someone called the boat an "O'Nealovich."

People lined up to get an O'Neal-built boat. The second boat to come out of O'Neal Boat Works was the 37-foot *Mel-O-Dee,* built for Buddy Cannady, now a boat-building legend on Roanoke Island. By 1964 O'Neal had built his third charter boat for a local fisherman, plus a custom yacht, his personal favorite, the *Lady B* for Marvin Blount of Greenville.

In 1964, O'Neal built a boat for himself, this time incorporating new construction techniques. On the *Pearl II* he followed his basic hull design but incorporated scarf planking and epoxy gluing, and this became the standard building technique in the area. After that, he built numerous custom yachts, including a series for angler John Wood, all named the *Olive E.*

O'Neal's boat designs were an amalgam of styles, a blend of influences that suited the users. He combined the Rybovich components of a shearline and S-frame with the flared bow that the Harkers Island boat builders used. O'Neal's innovation and contribution were to put these elements together and add a sharper entry, or more deadrise, at the forefoot of the keel. At the same time, he kept the stern nearly flat to give the boat more stability in rocking seas.

Boat building for O'Neal was about intuition and trial and error. He gave careful thought to the needs of a fishing boat on the Outer Banks, based on firsthand knowledge. He used the boats, rode in them, listened to the captains talk about how they operated, then refined each one. It was his habit to build scaled-down models of the boats before he built them, so he could see how they would turn out in advance.

Over time, O'Neal's boats got progressively sharper at the entry to the water, with up to 20 degrees of deadrise, a feature that allowed the boats to run faster with less horsepower through headseas. "I started putting the V in the hulls of the bigger boats because it seemed to me like they needed it," O'Neal told a reporter in 1991. "I had been running boats all my life and I knew what it took to make them run."

O'Neal's blend of borrowed elements created a style all his own, a style that influenced a whole generation of coastal Carolina boat builders and is visible in nearly every Carolina boat produced today. There are more than a dozen builders on Roanoke Island now, all working from O'Neal's basic bottom design. "He made a great impact," says Tillett. "He got boat building going. He was one of the first that made the change in the style of the boat."

O'Neal both fished and built boats for several years until he finally sold the *Pearl II* (it's now called the *Sinbad)* and went into boat building full time. O'Neal Boat Works on Dough's Creek was the first full-time boat building shop on the Outer Banks. Many of the most well-known Carolina boat builders got their start working at O'Neal Boat Works. In fact, Tillett went on to build several much-admired boats until his allergies to epoxy forced him to stop.

"Cap'n Warren started it all," well-known Roanoke Island boat builder Buddy Davis told a newspaper reporter in 1987. "He deserves a lot of the credit. The rest of us have taken the ball and run with it. But we've all worked from his basic design." Today's Carolina boats have evolved tremendously, as each builder takes liberties and adds his own signature to the basic hull design. But that's a whole other story!

O'Neal retired in the late 1970s and closed the doors on his boat shop for good. The last boat he built was a small 20-foot outboard for his grandson, similar to the first boat he built with his brother when he was young. His boat-building career had come full circle.

The Death of an Outer Banks Town

· 1971 ·

*Henry Pigott, 74, the last permanent male resident
on Portsmouth Island, died Tuesday [January 5,
1971] in the Albemarle General Hospital, Elizabeth
City, N.C. The funeral service was conducted at
10 A.M. Thursday in the Methodist Church on
Portsmouth. Mr. Pigott was buried in the cemetery
plot at the rear of the Babb home near the
church. . . . Mr. Pigott, who was born on
Portsmouth, leaves no immediate survivors.*

The obituary marked a milestone, not just in the life of a
man but in the life of an island. Mr. Henry Pigott, a descendant
of slaves who was born on Portsmouth Island in 1896, who had
spent all seventy-four years of his life fishing on the island, was
gone. The island would never be the same.

With his death, only two residents remained in the tiny village on Portsmouth Island. Marian Gray Babb and Elma Dixon,
both getting on in years, had a decision to make. Though they
spent their winters on the mainland, the two women spent the
majority of their year on Portsmouth, enjoying the island life.
Would they be able to stay without Mr. Henry there to help

them? They decided not. Dixon and Babb reluctantly packed up their belongings and left their island homes in 1971, moving across the Core Sound to the mainland community of Beaufort.

Thus, Portsmouth was deserted. The homes were lifeless, their porches devoid of rockers, and their yards overgrown. The organ and the bell at the Methodist Church were silent. The post office boxes, not used since 1959, were full of cobwebs and dust. The desks at the schoolhouse and the bunks at the Coast Guard station sat empty. All that remained were signs that there had once been a thriving village here, but there was no one left to tell the stories of the rise and fall of Portsmouth.

Portsmouth, on Core Banks just across Ocracoke Inlet from Ocracoke Island, was the first planned village on the Outer Banks and was once the most populated. The North Carolina Colonial Assembly created Portsmouth in 1753, making it an official town with an official name before there was any building or being there. The Colonial Assembly authorized the town because there was a dire need for shipping facilities on the south side of Ocracoke Inlet. (At first, Portsmouth was just the name of a village on Core Banks, a long stretch of island from Ocracoke Inlet to Beaufort Inlet. Later, in the 1930s when Drum Inlet opened, the village of Portsmouth sat on its own small island, which became known as Portsmouth Island.)

At the time, the towns of northeastern and central North Carolina—Bath, New Bern, Washington, and Edenton among them—depended on Ocracoke Inlet for the transport of import and export cargo like sugar, spices, lumber, and fabric. Ocracoke Inlet was the only safe passageway between the Atlantic Ocean and these inland communities. But getting big ships laden with cargo through Ocracoke Inlet was difficult. The inlet was shallow, and vessels would have to unload much of their ballast and cargo onto small "lightering" boats to get through the inlet. Once the ships had made it safely into deeper waters, the lightering crews would help them load their cargo back on board. The main channel through the inlet was on the south side, nearer to Core Banks than to Ocracoke. The Colonial Assembly envisioned a town on Core Banks that could ease the shipping predicaments through Ocracoke Inlet.

The Colonial Assembly mandated that the purchasers of the lots on Portsmouth were to build "good, substantial, habitable" framed or brick houses or warehouses within eighteen months of purchase. The first man bought a lot in 1756.

For nearly a century, Portsmouth was one of the Outer Banks' largest and most important communities. Two-thirds of the state's exports passed through the Ocracoke Inlet in the early 1800s, and the residents of Portsmouth Village were there to lighter the ships and serve the sailors. The town's population in 1810 had climbed to 387. There were two churches, a school, an academy, a custom's house, naval stores, warehouses, several privately owned stores, a barroom and, by 1840, a post office. So many vessels passed through Ocracoke Inlet—records from 1836–1837 showed more than 1,400 vessels in a year's time—that the government established a Seafarer's Hospital on the island. Sick sailors coming from long journeys at sea were treated or quarantined on Portsmouth Island.

Portsmouth was a thriving community. The village hit its peak in 1850, when there were 100 buildings and 505 people, of whom 117 were slaves. It's said that the homes were well kept, always freshly painted with neat lawns. Livestock, such as cows, horses, sheep, and pigs, freely roamed the island, keeping the island's natural vegetation trim. "Everything on the island was so clean, I have been told that a man could wear a white shirt for a week without getting it soiled for there was no dust and dirt on this island," wrote Ben Salter in his book called *Portsmouth Island Short Stories and History.*

But the winds of prosperity began to shift for Portsmouth Island. The sea, weather, and changing times altered the island's purpose, and people began leaving the island, one by one.

The first problem was Ocracoke Inlet. It started shoaling and became a much less dependable passageway. When

Hatteras Inlet opened to the north in 1846, shipping traffic started using that inlet instead. During the Civil War, with the approach of Union soldiers, many of the island residents fled to the mainland. By the end of the Civil War, all of the shipping traffic on the Outer Banks had switched to using Hatteras Inlet instead of Ocracoke Inlet, and there was no reason for many of those who had fled to come back.

By 1870 the population of Portsmouth was 320, and by 1880 it had trickled down to 220. Shipping and lightering were out, and the only way to make a living was to fish. A menhaden processing plant nearby on Casey Island provided work for the locals, but it was destroyed in the terrible hurricane of 1899. Fortunately, a U.S. Lifesaving Station had opened in 1894, which provided good jobs and a reason for a few families to stay on the island.

The people who remained on Portsmouth Island lived a quiet life. They went to church and school, harbored shipwrecked sailors and salvaged shipwrecked goods, gathered fresh seafood from the sea and vegetables from their gardens, and raised livestock. Getting mail and supplies from the mail boat and infrequent trips to Ocracoke were some of the highlights of life. Many former residents have written, quite nostalgically, about the joys of such free and simple living. Yet while life was simple, it was never easy. The island never had telephones or electricity, though a few people had generators in later years. There was no refrigeration, only dairy houses kept mildly cool by sea breezes. Separate kitchens, outhouses, mosquitoes, and harsh weather were a way of life.

The elements were—and still are—harsh on Portsmouth Island. When the Civilian Conservation Corps built oceanfront dunes along the Outer Banks in the 1930s, they didn't go as far as the Core Banks. Left in its natural state, the island is flat from sea to sound, and the "sea tide" often floods into the village. Compounding this problem in the early days was the fact that free-roaming livestock kept the natural vegetation low, preventing any sort of barrier dunes from forming between the village and the ocean. Salt flats and low marsh surround the village, and the buildings are built on the highest points of land possible, but this doesn't prevent frequent flooding from both the sound and ocean sides.

When the Lifesaving Station, which changed hands to the Coast Guard in 1915, was decommissioned in 1937, Portsmouth's population began to decline even more. The 1930 census listed 104 residents, but by 1956 there were only 17 residents, and the only thing you could buy on the island was a postage stamp. The post office finally closed in 1959. In 1970 there were just three residents left on Portsmouth Island, and in 1971 they were all gone.

But the Outer Banks ghost town has not been forgotten. In 1976 the National Park Service established the Cape Lookout National Seashore, taking over all of North and South Core Banks and Shackleford Banks, including Portsmouth Island and the deserted village of Portsmouth. Twenty structures, including the 1914 Methodist Church, the 1920 school, the late-1700s Washington Roberts House, the 1840s post office, and many others, have been preserved, either by the National Park Service or by a few individuals with leases to use the homes in return for upkeep. Seasonal caretakers volunteer their time during each warm season to watch over the island and its buildings, but there are no full-time residents and no electricity, and it is accessible only by boat from Ocracoke or the mainland. In some ways, the decline of Portsmouth village has been a blessing. Now a part of the National Park Service, the village is forever preserved in time, one of the few remaining vestiges of a historic Outer Banks village.

Discovering the
Monitor
• 1973 •

The water off the coast of North Carolina contains the nation's highest concentration of shipwrecks. Often called the Graveyard of the Atlantic, it is an underwater archaeologist's dream. The ocean floor in this aquatic underworld bears the skeletal remnants and hulks of hundreds of sunken ships—four centuries worth of schooners, frigates, clippers, sloops, brigantines, cargo ships, gunboats, steamers, lightships, blockade runners, tugs, barges, tankers, submarines, U-boats, and yachts. Some are too far gone to ever be identified, but others are just waiting to be discovered by anyone willing to explore the depths of the sea.

One of the most fascinating ships at rest in the Graveyard of the Atlantic is the USS *Monitor,* the innovative nineteenth-century gunboat designed specifically for sea battles. Launched by the Union Navy in 1862, the steam-powered, turreted, iron-clad ship was famous for its Civil War battle with the CSS *Virginia,* a definitive battle that ended the era of wooden-hulled, sailing warships. The 172-foot-long ship, constructed almost entirely of iron, was the first ship to have a revolving turret as well as the first to have engines and living space below the water line.

The *Monitor* sank off the coast of Cape Hatteras on New Year's Eve of the same year it was launched. Though its lifespan was less than a year, the *Monitor* was nevertheless one of the most significant ships in naval history because it was incredibly innovative in its time.

The exact location of the great ship's resting place was unknown for 111 years, but it wasn't for lack of trying to find it. As soon as technology advanced to the point that deepwater exploration became possible, oceanographers, underwater archaeologists, divers, historians, and shipwreck enthusiasts spent three decades looking for the *Monitor*.

The first possible discovery occurred in 1945, when a team performing tests with a UOL (underwater object locator) found a 140-foot-long object on the ocean floor. However, divers were never able to get close enough to identify the wreck because of strong currents. Subsequent years saw the founding of the USS Monitor Foundation, with an offer of a $1,000 reward for anyone who could locate the *Monitor*. Then there was the Marine who claimed he had found the ship in shallow water but could never find it again, and the group who claimed to have found the turret but lost the buoy marking the location.

In 1973 the search resumed with a well-funded and promising expedition. John G. Newton, marine superintendent for the oceanographic program at the Duke Marine Laboratory, led a highly skilled team of scientists whose primary purpose was to test geological survey equipment. They planned to map a specific area of the continental shelf off the North Carolina coast, but the team also wanted to test the equipment's usefulness for underwater archaeology. They decided they would also look for the shipwrecked *Monitor,* which would be easily identifiable because of its unique characteristics.

On board Duke University's 100-foot research vessel *Eastward,* Newton's expedition left Beaufort, North Carolina, in August 1973. The plan was to retrace the path of the USS *Rhode Island,* the side-wheel steamer that was towing the *Monitor* the night she sank. Using an 1857 coast survey chart and the *Rhode Island's* logbook, the *Eastward* followed the ships' route around the dreaded Diamond Shoals off Cape Hatteras, the heart of the Graveyard of the Atlantic.

It was at Diamond Shoals on New Year's Eve in 1862 that the *Monitor* began taking on water. En route to South Carolina to battle the Confederates, the powerful *Rhode Island* was towing the *Monitor* to make the journey faster. As the ships rounded Cape Hatteras the winds increased to gale force and water washed into the *Monitor* through a leak in the turret.

For fear of striking its tow ship, the *Monitor's* commander ordered the tow lines to be cut. This was done, but the lines became entangled in the *Rhode Island's* wheel, rendering that ship immobile. The *Monitor's* anchor was ordered dropped, but as it went down the anchor well sprang a leak. With the ocean washing in faster than they could bail, the *Monitor's* crew sent up a red light signal, the sign that they were abandoning their ship. Two life boats from the *Rhode Island* came to rescue them, and the *Monitor* sank to the bottom. Sixteen men were lost.

Aboard the *Eastward* in 1973, Newton's team painstakingly searched a 5-mile by 14-mile section of the Atlantic floor with sonar equipment. Locating twenty-one wrecks, the researchers compared each one with the known characteristics of the *Monitor* but none matched its description. On the last day of research, August 27, the side-scan sonar recorded a "long, amorphous echo" that indicated the discovery of a twenty-second wreck, 16 miles south-southeast of the Cape Hatteras Lighthouse.

Lying in 220 feet of water, the shipwreck was difficult to study. The scientists dangled underwater video and still cameras on cables from their research vessel then navigated back and forth over the site. The resulting black-and-whites images, fuzzy and unclear though they were, looked promising. Though the ship was upside down, the scientists could see a flat, unobstructed surface similar to the *Monitor's* hull, a thick waist that could possibly be its armor belt, and a circular structure that resembled the turret.

For the next five months, researchers studied the images and compared them with historical documents. In March 1974, Newton announced to the world that he had found the *Monitor.*

A month later Newton and a research team went back to the site a second time to verify the find. Aboard the sophisticated *Alcoa Seaprobe,* a vessel specifically designed for deep-ocean exploration and recovery, the team had access to better equipment, including side- and forward-looking sonar, television cameras with flood lights, and two deep-sea 35mm cameras with strobe lights. More than 1,200 photographs, several hours of videotape, and a photomosaic proved that this was indeed the *Monitor.*

On January 30, 1975, the *Monitor* and the column of water surrounding it, 1 nautical mile in diameter, were named as the first U.S. National Marine Sanctuary. Management of the wreck site by the National Oceanic and Atmospheric Administration (NOAA) focuses on recovery of artifacts and protecting the ship from damage by anchors, fishing, or divers. The site is closed to deep-sea divers unless they have a difficult-to-obtain federal permit, which is often a point of contention in the diving community. The *Monitor* is also on the National Historic Register and is a National Historic Landmark.

Diving and recovering artifacts at the site has been difficult. In a location where the Gulf Stream interacts with the Labrador Current, eddies, currents, weather, and visibility are unpredictable and instantly changeable. Nevertheless, none of that has deterred NOAA from recovering artifacts from the *Monitor.* NOAA expeditions between 1977 and 1983 recovered a brass lantern, the 1,500-pound anchor, and a series of small artifacts. In 1988 the propeller and propeller shaft were lifted out of the ocean. In August 2002 recovery crews, including NOAA scientists and one hundred elite Navy divers, used cranes to raise the ship's 120-ton gun turret, one of the heaviest artifacts ever recovered from the sea floor.

The gun turret, the most unique of the boat's features, was 22 feet in diameter, 9 feet high, contained two cannon, and was clad in eight layers of thick iron plates to protect the crew members inside. The gun turret revolved on the ship, allowing for an enormous range of fire. When the turret was brought into the light of day for the first time since the ship sank, the scientists found several items used in warfare, including ramrods and sponges for the cannon and copper ladles used to unload gun powder. But they also found some very curious and strangely placed artifacts. Inside the turret were sterling silver utensils, ivory-handled knives with engraved initials, shoes, leather straps, wooden pulley blocks, a wool overcoat, buttons, coins, a comb, and part of a wooden cabinet.

At first these finds confounded the scientists, but soon their positioning became obvious. When the ship was upright, the gun turret was on the deck above the storage units and the galley. With the ship resting upside down, the storage units were above the turret. As time went by, these items trickled from the hull into the turret.

Also in the recovered turret were the remains of two crew members. Accounts of the night the *Monitor* sank told of the turret being the last part of the ship above the water, with sailors clinging to it for their lives.

The *Monitor* is slowly deteriorating in its saltwater grave. After more than 140 years of soaking in oxygen-rich water, the iron body is corroding, vulnerable and riddled with holes. But its great hulk is not a useless wasteland at the bottom of the sea. In its reincarnation as an artificial reef, the ship is host to a variety of sea life, including amberjack, black sea bass, red barbier, sand tiger sharks, dolphin, corals, sea anemones, and sea urchins.

Many of the items recovered from the ship are on display in the Mariners' Museum in Newport News, Virginia, and will soon be on display on the Outer Banks at the new Graveyard of the Atlantic Museum in Hatteras Village.

How to Save
a Sand Dune
• 1973 •

*Save the dunes. They belong to the people. They
represent the signature of time and eternity.
Their loss would be irrevocable.*
—Carl Sandburg

On August 15, 1973, the guttural drone of a bulldozer
broke the stillness of the early morning and fell on the ears of
a few residents and summer visitors in Nags Head. Carolista
and Walter Baum, whose summer house and jewelry business
were located on the Beach Road in Nags Head, thought the
sound was coming from the direction of Jockey's Ridge, the
giant sand dune they climbed with their three children nearly
every day. They got dressed and headed out to investigate.

Tramping through the soft sand in the morning sun, the
Baums made it to the top of the highest dune ridge and
scanned the surrounding area for the source of the noise. At the
north base of the dunes they spotted a bright yellow bulldozer
grading a low hill. Plumes of black smoke emitted into the air
as the bulldozer leveled the sand.

Carolista felt a surge of protectiveness for her beloved
dunes. Just weeks before she was outraged when an out-of-
town landowner had placed a FOR SALE sign on a highly visible
parcel of property on Jockey's Ridge. Without hesitation, Car-

olista marched directly up to the massive yellow beast and planted herself in its path. To the driver's surprise, the young woman refused to move to allow him to finish his work. When her tenacity became apparent, he stopped the engines, climbed down, and left. According to local lore, Carolista reportedly then removed a part from the bulldozer's engine to keep it shut down for a while.

It was a temporary halt to development on Jockey's Ridge.

Jockey's Ridge is the largest naturally formed sand dune in the eastern United States. The great golden mountain rises up from the surrounding landscape—the dense foliage of Nags Head Woods to the north, the Roanoke Sound to the west, and resort-town development of Nags Head to the south and east—into a high, surreal, seemingly misplaced desert. The dune is and always has been the focal point of Nags Head. Generations of residents and visitors have prowled its peaks, climbing to the highest point for a view of both the sound and the ocean, to witness sunrises, sunsets, and stars, to run downhill in sand-filled shoes, or to fly off the top in hang-gliders.

To the Baums and many other people of the Outer Banks, Jockey's Ridge had always been public land. Everyone used it as if it was a giant public park, but in actuality the sands of Jockey's Ridge were the property of two dozen private landowners. Ownership and public use of Jockey's Ridge had never been an issue until the late 1960s, when land values in Nags Head increased to the point where the grains of sand were actually worth some money.

In 1972, when a landowner developed a northern tract of the dunes into a condominium complex known as The Villas, the people of Nags Head became concerned about the fate of Jockey's Ridge. Historically there had been a number of similar prominent sand hills and ridges in the area of Nags Head—the Round-About Hills, Scraggly Oak Hill, Graveyard Hill, Engagement Hill, Pin Hill, and the Seven Sisters—but these were no longer recognizable because of development or because their sand had been removed for use at other locations.

Carolista Baum didn't want to see Jockey's Ridge suffer a similar fate. Her stalwart act of bulldozer-blocking in August 1973 was, by itself, not enough to save Jockey's Ridge, but it is the unique, memorable image that has lived on as the beginning of the effort. In actuality, people had been trying to save the dunes a decade before the incident, and it would take many more people and several more years to preserve Jockey's Ridge once and for all.

In 1964 local author David Stick, during his swearing-in ceremony as president of the Outer Banks Chamber of Commerce, announced that one of his main goals was the acquisition of Jockey's Ridge for placement in the public domain. While he had support in the beginning, this early effort failed because of the difficulty of establishing ownership for some of the land and the reluctance of landowners to sell at a time when land prices were just beginning to rise. The Town of Nags Head had also made early efforts to preserve Jockey's Ridge. In its first Land Use Plan in 1964, the town stated that it wished to create a park at Jockey's Ridge, but no immediate action was taken.

In 1972, when the Villas Condominiums had been approved for the base of the ridge and the project was in the earth-moving stages, local residents Philip Quidley and Henry Applewhite started the Friends of Jockey's Ridge and sent out a wave of telegrams to conservation-minded organizations and the press. It wasn't enough to stop the condominium development, but it did get the attention of the North Carolina Board of Conservation and Development, bringing the issue out into the open. Suddenly people were thinking about what needed to be done. The Town of Nags Head, in September 1972, drafted a resolution calling for the preservation of Jockey's Ridge.

The town's resolution brought immediate action from the state, which sent State Parks Director Thomas Ellis to meet with

Nags Head Mayor Carl Nunemaker. Ellis told Nunemaker that in order to preserve Jockey's Ridge and designate it a state park, they would need at least 400 acres. He also said there was no money for the project and admitted that the state would not likely take the lead in preserving the dune. The leadership for the project, he said, would have to come from the town.

After that meeting, Nunemaker did two things. First, he organized the passing of a town ordinance that prevented the removal of sand from Jockey's Ridge for use at other locations, and secondly, he spoke to the one person that he knew could spearhead such a local campaign: a vivacious artist and activist with a strong personality, Carolista Baum. One year later, her bulldozer sit-in was the perfect dramatic start to get the locals involved.

The bulldozer work that Carolista interrupted was part of a second condominium development project. The Baums learned that the Town of Nags Head was already in the process of seeking state park status for Jockey's Ridge and town officials were planning to meet with the North Carolina Board of Conservation and Development at the end of August. At a meeting at the Town of Nags Head offices on August 19, 1973, Carolista and Walter Baum volunteered to circulate a petition calling for park status for Jockey's Ridge. The petition's theme was "SOS. Save Our Sand Dune," and Carolista set out to get 30,000 signatures in two weeks.

She printed 500 copies of her "SOS" petition, recruited her friends and neighbors, and got to work. Within days they had collected 25,000 signatures. She presented the petition to the Board of Conservation and Development when they met with the Town of Nags Head officials in August 1973. In true Carolista fashion, she also pulled at the board members' heart strings, playing a recording of the song "A Natural High—The Ballad of Jockey's Ridge" by local band Russ & Us. The meeting went well. The board expressed a real interest in preserving Jockey's Ridge as a state park, and State Parks Director Ellis promised swift action on the initiative.

Carolista Fletcher Baum had grown up in nearby Edenton in a prominent family, who had nicknamed her "Tootsie," and she had spent every summer of her life in Nags Head. She was the perfect figurehead for the local effort to save Jockey's Ridge. With a pretty face and big smile she was likeable and approachable, with charm, enthusiasm, determination, and spunk. Her petition, along with her personality, captured the attention of state legislators and the people of the Outer Banks.

"Carolista came from a well-connected local family," said Marlene Roberts, who volunteered full-time for eighteen months in the effort to save Jockey's Ridge. "She had the ability to pick up the phone and talk to influential people. It was nothing for her to be friendly with the governor."

Though the efforts to save Jockey's Ridge had been going on for almost a decade, Carolista was able to immediately garner a great deal of attention and to create a sense of urgency about saving the Nags Head landmark. "Carolista was a young, vivacious, exciting person," former husband Walter Baum said in 2003. "She captured attention easily. But we were the johnny-come-latelies. We came into the right place at the right time, when there was an explosion of local interest."

Carolista Baum threw herself wholeheartedly into the effort of saving Jockey's Ridge. She formed the nonprofit People To Preserve Jockey's Ridge (PTPJR), filled the board of directors with just the right blend of wealthy and prominent people, and used her Nags Head jewelry store as headquarters. In winter, when she and her family moved back to Chapel Hill, her efforts didn't stop. She consulted with local and state leaders about plans of action. She and other Outer Banks residents lobbied influential state politicians. After an extensive lobbying jag by Carolista and many others in April 1974, the state legislature appropriated $500,000 for land acquisition at Jockey's Ridge.

Meanwhile, the Town of Nags Head did what it could to legally stop development of Jockey's Ridge. And in July 1974, the Department of the Interior announced the inclusion of Jockey's Ridge in the National Registry of Natural Landmarks.

By the summer of 1974, PTPJR was in full swing. Many local people and organizations jumped on board to help and the organization grew to 13,000 members. Schoolchildren held fund-raisers with SOS bookmarks, posters, and bumper stickers. The Outer Banks Women's Club, headed by Marlene Roberts, addressed and mailed 10,000 brochures about the movement to save Jockey's Ridge. Save Our Sand Dune T-shirts, balloons, posters, records, kites, placemats, and bumper stickers were seen everywhere. Though the PTPJR effort made incredible strides in raising awareness of the issue, it actually did little fund-raising. After one year of incorporation, the organization was in the hole by more than $800. Carolista, undaunted, forged ahead with a letter-writing campaign and secured a few small grants toward land acquisition.

A bigger boon to the Jockey's Ridge project was The Nature Conservancy's purchase of sixty acres of the dunes, which would eventually be donated to become part of the state park. Over the course of the next year, Nags Head and Outer Banks officials also did everything they could to get the state park approved.

Finally, on April 12, 1975, the North Carolina Council of State unanimously voted to buy 196.8 acres of Jockey's Ridge land for $1.3 million. In conjunction with The Nature Conservancy's purchase and some private land donations, this action assured that Jockey's Ridge would be preserved. (An additional 140 acres for the park were later purchased with funds from the federal Bureau of Outdoor Recreation.)

Ever the optimist, Carolista Baum wanted to have the Jockey's Ridge State Park celebration party by June 1, 1975. She pushed the state to establish Jockey's Ridge as a state park even before the land purchases were completed, and her three-day celebration took place as planned. The Jockey's Ridge Jamboree Weekend started on May 31, 1975, even though at the time the state did not own any land on Jockey's Ridge. The event featured a hang-gliding competition, fireworks, a fish fry, benefit dances, school bands, the official announcement of the ridge as a National Natural Landmark, dedication ceremonies, and a barefoot march to the summit of the dune led by Natural and Economic Resources Office Director Jim Harrington.

It was the work of many that led to Jockey's Ridge's preservation, but after thirty years it is Carolista who stands out in most people's minds as the legendary champion of Jockey's Ridge. The conservation of Jockey's Ridge would have happened without Carolista Baum, but the excitement and urgency of the project wouldn't have been there without her. She made the campaign to "Save Our Sand Dune" memorable. Carolista passed away in 1991 at age fifty.

Today Jockey's Ridge State Park preserves 420 acres, including three dune peaks that form a *medaño* (shifting sands without vegetation), pockets of maritime thicket, and Roanoke Sound shores. It harbors more than eighty species of plants, several species of mammals and reptiles, and hundreds of species of birds. More than one million visitors visit the park every year.

"The Ship Hit the Span"
• 1990 •

At about 6:00 P.M. on October 25, 1990, Capt. William O. Cliett decided to quit dredging and call it a day. The sea was becoming rough and the forecast called for thirty- to thirty-five-knot winds out of the north-northeast later that night. Cliett and his nine-man crew eased the dredge to the anchoring spot they always chose for those forecasted conditions and dropped anchor a quarter-mile east of the Bonner Bridge. The ten men went about their normal after-work activities aboard their 3,500-ton floating island of steel, the 194-foot dredge *Northerly Isle.*

Within hours of anchoring the *Northerly Isle,* Captain Cliett got a queasy feeling. The flat-hulled ship was pounding on the waves and straining against the weight of the anchor. Keeping a constant eye on the weather conditions, he learned things were much worse than the forecast had predicted. The winds picked up to 45 to 55 knots, with even stronger gusts, and the seas were at 3 to 5 feet. A 6-knot tidal current surged through the inlet. He certainly hadn't imagined a storm this bad. Staring out the cockpit windows into the dark storm, he mentally marked his ship's positioning in comparison with the bright light of a buoy not far from his anchorage.

The *Northerly Isle's* crew was stationed at Oregon Inlet, removing sand from the channel as part of an ongoing effort to keep a consistent depth in the East Coast's most notoriously shoaling inlet. Mammoth, bargelike dredges are a mainstay at Oregon Inlet, part of the U.S. Army Corps of Engineers' struggle to keep the inlet safe and passable as the inlet fills in with sand, a natural process called shoaling. The dredges suck sand out of the inlet and displace it to another location. Millions of dollars are spent each year in this ongoing battle against the building and shifting shoals.

At 10:30 P.M., Cliett returned to the cockpit and witnessed a disheartening sight. The lighted buoy he had been monitoring as his location marker was dimmer than before. He realized in a dread-filled instant that the current and winds had forced the ship's sole anchor free of its hold in the sand. The anchor was dragging bottom, and the ship was moving through the inlet, toward the bridge.

Cliett knew what he had to do. He ordered everyone into life jackets and called for the engines to be brought to full power in an effort to fight the dredge's westward drift. Moments later they struck a shoal, which grounded the dredge about 250 yards east of the bridge. It was probably the only time a ship's captain had been ecstatic upon running aground in Oregon Inlet. Cliett ordered the crew to pump the ballast tanks full of water, hoping that the extra weight would keep the *Northerly Isle* grounded for the duration of the storm.

But it wasn't to be. The current ate away at the shoal, slipping it right out from under the ship's hull. Overpowered by Mother Nature, the *Northerly Isle* drifted westward again. At 12:50 A.M. the dredge was a mere 200 feet from the bridge.

At 1:10 A.M., Cliett notified the Oregon Inlet Coast Guard Station. Close the bridge to traffic, he told them.

Twenty minutes later, with a thunderous clash of concrete and steel, the stern of the *Northerly Isle* slammed into the pilings of the Herbert C. Bonner Bridge. The portside bow soon followed. Over and over again, the dredge rammed into the bridge, driven by relentless wind and tide.

With bridge spans buckling above them and chunks of concrete threatening to fall on the ship, four of the crew members escaped. They scrambled to the top of the ship's wheelhouse, which was almost level with the bridge's railings, climbed over the railings, and ran down the bridge toward land.

"As I started across the front of the house, the dredge banged into the bridge again," Ronald Shaw, the cook, later wrote. "The port running light sheared off and fell. I watched [it] drop. Saw the bridge stanchion crack. I ran up the deck, up … onto the bridge and ran like hell down the bridge to the police car."

The Dare County sheriff's department deputies were waiting on either side of the span. Deputy Thaddeous Pledger had arrived on the north end just as the dredge began to pound at the bridge. Pledger could see the bridge moving, the spans bowing, but he knew he had to get to the south side to stop the traffic. He jumped in his car and gunned the gas pedal to the floor, speeding safely across the buckling spans to the south side of the bridge. He returned by foot to the collision site to find four crew men climbing over the railings. One ran his way, the rest ran north.

At 2:30 A.M. on October 26, the bridge collapsed. Three hundred and seventy feet of the two-lane bridge fell into the inlet.

"Every time the barge would hit the bridge, the bridge would bow out," Pledger told a *Virginian-Pilot* reporter. "At first it was like little dips, and then one flap (of concrete) fell, and then another." Electrical cables that ran the length of the bridge ruptured and exploded with a show of fireworks in the dark.

Miraculously, no one was hurt, nor was the dredge. The remaining men were rescued from the *Northerly Isle* and the dredge was towed to Norfolk after the storm. A particularly creative newspaper editor ran the headline "The Ship Hit the Span."

But the 5,000 residents of Hatteras Island were suddenly stranded on their own island. Their tangible link to the rest of the world was severed, as was their power and phone service. Locals couldn't get to work "up the beach" in Manteo and Nags Head. Unless they left the island on a crowded ferry to Ocracoke, everyone was stuck on Hatteras Island.

It took nine days to establish car ferry service across Oregon Inlet. A pedestrian-only ferry—an old World War II–style landing craft—had transported people across the inlet just days after the accident, but the first car ferry carried the first twenty-two cars across on November 7.

It took an hour of zigzagging around shoals to get the ferries between Hatteras and Bodie Islands. Though the inlet is only about 2½ miles wide, the ferry's path was 6½ miles long, through the deep waters of Walter Slough and Old House Channel. The ferries ran twenty-four hours day, struggling to pass each other in the narrow channels and sometimes running aground.

Before the Bonner Bridge was completed in 1963, leisurely ferry rides were the traditional means of crossing the inlet. But thirty years later, people who were used to zipping across the Oregon Inlet bridge in about three minutes found the hour-long ferry ride excruciating.

Hatteras's usually vibrant autumn economy plummeted. The ferries couldn't carry nearly as many people as the bridge had funneled over in a day. The year before, the bridge had carried up to 4,000 people a day to Hatteras Island; the ferries could do 1,100 at best. Charter fishing boats sat in the docks, while restaurants, motels, and shops were empty. The wait for the ferry line was sometimes hours long. Life without the bridge was hard.

The residents of Hatteras Island learned all too well what life was like when their lifeline—the seemingly indestructible Herbert C. Bonner Bridge over Oregon Inlet—was cut in one quick moment. This hardship was a reminder that bridges are the lifelines of barrier islands. The residents of Hatteras Island and the northern Outer Banks are dependent on their bridges, not only for economic reasons but also for safety and efficiency. The massive structures of concrete, steel, and asphalt support entire island communities and their established ways of life.

It took about four months to rebuild the Bonner Bridge. In mid-February of 1991, the residents of Hatteras Island rejoiced when the bridge again opened up their island to the world.

In the year following the accident, some people tried to put the blame of the accident on Captain Cliett. An extensive investigation of the incident followed, but in the end, he was not charged with negligence. In October 1991, a judge ruled that the catastrophe was the "direct result of an act of God." As is proven so often on the Outer Banks, man has little power in the face of Mother Nature.

Wild but Not As Free
• 1995 •

Munching contentedly on a manicured lawn in Corolla, the black stallion was indifferent to the human activity around him: people walking past, cars and delivery trucks speeding by on Highway 12, construction crews hammering away on million-dollar vacation homes. But then, looking up into the morning light with a mouthful of grass, the horse was startled by the sight of two riders on horseback headed straight for him. He bolted off the lawn, running full-speed through a nearby construction site, around the house, and past the workers who stopped to watch the scene. The riders tailed close to the horse, while a truck closed in ahead of him. The stallion's only possible path left him trapped between a row of sand fence and his pursuers. With no other recourse, he gave up the chase.

His captors treated the horse gently, nudging him northward, away from the vacation homes, the tender green lawns, and, most importantly, the cars. They steered him past the end of the paved road to the wildlife refuge, behind a wood-and-wire fence built especially to contain the wild horses of Corolla.

The rest of that day—March 25, 1995—the modern-day cowboys, who were volunteers with the Corolla Wild Horse Fund, pursued other horses through the village and resort subdivisions, around swimming pools and tennis courts, across the golf course, through yards and over fences. They flushed them out of hiding places beneath trees and behind dunes. They followed one horse all the way to the village of Duck, 12 miles south. At the end of the day they had corralled fourteen horses, but it was a tough job. The horses did not want to leave what had been their home, and they employed every trick they knew to avoid it.

The wild horses of the Currituck Outer Banks had never known anything but complete freedom. They roamed the barrier island from southern Virginia to the village of Duck, even as community settlements, a lighthouse, lifesaving stations, hunt clubs, roads and, later, shopping centers and thousands of vacation houses sprang up in their grazing grounds.

It is widely believed that the Corolla wild horses, like those on Ocracoke Island and Shackleford Banks farther south, have been living on the northern Outer Banks for more than 400 years, since the era of early Spanish and English exploration of the New World. It is unknown exactly how the horses arrived on this coast, but most believe it was by way of Spanish or English explorers, or perhaps both. Spanish conquistadors explored coastal North Carolina in the early 1500s, bringing with them horses, sheep, cows, and pigs that were bred in the Spanish colony of Puerto Rico, but they abandoned their livestock when they ran into conflict with the Native Americans. Later, English explorers brought Spanish-bred horses and livestock on their voyages to the New World between 1584 and 1590. Some say the horses could have also swum ashore from shipwrecks. Scientific and genetic studies have proven that the horses have genetic connections to Spanish mustangs. In fact, they are some of the purest descendants of the Spanish mustangs because of their isolation on the remote Outer Banks.

However the horses got to the North Carolina coast, they were well established on the Currituck Outer Banks by the early 1700s, when English historian John Lawson explored the area. For the next 300 years, the horses coexisted harmoniously with the scant population of humans on the island.

In the 1980s and 1990s, however, the Corolla area mushroomed into a vacation resort and thousands of people began visiting the area. The horses' longtime habitat became dangerous to them, and they became dangerous to others. After the road between Duck and Corolla was paved in 1984, horses and cars collided. Thirty-two horses were killed by cars between 1984 and 1995, nearly decimating the herd.

Though the horses were in danger amidst the traffic, they were quite content with the new nature of things. The sod lawns and landscaped plants were much more tender and delicious than their normal diet of bitter, coarse weeds and marsh grasses. Plus there were lots of tasty new foods for them to try, namely scraps from trash cans and handouts from unwary tourists. A few horses took to hanging around the grocery store parking lot, where some soft-hearted person would usually come along and buy them an apple or a carrot.

The tourists loved seeing the wild horses roaming through the community. The bay, chestnut, sorrel, and black wild horses were a beautiful sight grazing right alongside the roads and in the neighborhoods. But many visitors didn't understand that the horses were wild animals. People were kicked or bitten when they tried to interact with the horses. The horses were hurt trying to find new things to eat; one horse was hurt falling off a deck after some people lured it upstairs for a bite of pizza. It soon became apparent that something would have to be done to protect the herd of wild horses.

In 1989 a group of local residents formed the Corolla Wild Horse Fund. They named and catalogued all of the horses and raised money to help protect them. The fund's volunteer directors devised a plan to move the horses to safer ground north of Corolla and contain them there with a fence. From the north of Corolla up to the Virginia border, the barrier island is a much different place than the rest of the Outer Banks. There is no paved road, and traffic is by four-wheel-drive vehicle only. In the early 1990s, there were only a few small enclaves of homes at Swan Beach, North Swan Beach, and Carova. It's a vast, remote, open expanse of private and public land, including the Currituck and Mackay Island National Wildlife Refuges. Many of the wild horses already lived in the territory, and there was plenty of room—about 17,000 acres—for the others who lived in Corolla.

By 1995 the Corolla Wild Horse Fund had raised more than $30,000, enough to build a horse fence. They secured a permit from the Army Corps of Engineers and built a mile-long, four-foot-high fence across the island from the sound to the ocean, right at the end of the paved road. An open area with a cattle grate allowed vehicles and pedestrians to pass through but not the horses. On March 25, 1995, any horses south of the fence were rounded up and moved north of the fence.

Within three days of being corralled behind the fence, a two-year-old chestnut colt named Sienna escaped. He wiggled under a sagging cable in the fence and galloped toward the greener pastures, but he was soon caught and herded back home. Another horse, a stallion named M&M, walked around the east end of the fence at low tide and eluded Horse Fund members for several days. Workers then lengthened the fence another twenty feet into the ocean to prevent further instances of skirting the fence at low tide.

One band of horses became particularly unruly, unable to resist Corolla's tasty treats. A stallion named Little Red Man, along with his harem of mares and colts, continually found a way around the fence, into garbage, and onto lawns, particularly the parklike lawn at The Whalehead Club. Once, Little Red Man's band even raided the local produce stand, causing more than $500 in damage. The Horse Fund had to bail them out. Finally, the Horse Fund penned Little Red Man and his harem near the Currituck Beach Lighthouse, but the horses kept escaping. In the summer of 1999, one of the mares and her eight-week-old colt escaped, and the mare was killed on the road near the lighthouse. The colt, called "Little Man," stood in the road looking at his mother's lifeless body for a long time. The headstrong band of horses was eventually moved to Dews Island in the Currituck Sound, where they have 400 acres of freedom. Little Man has been gentled and is now the Corolla Wild Horse Fund's ambassador, attending public events when he is called upon to do so.

The rest of the wild horses, seventy-six at this writing, are content on their 17,000-acre stomping grounds north of Corolla, where they feast on salt hay and coarse grasses and drink the rainwater that collects in the swales. A multi-agency management plan established in 2000 limits the number of wild horses in the area to sixty, so the Corolla Wild Horse Fund has to work to thin the herd by adopting out colts every year. When adopted young, the wild horses are easily tamed.

The fund, now with two part-time co-directors, protects the herd's safety and health, but they do not feed them or interfere with their natural habits. Horses occasionally still escape their boundaries, either into Virginia or Corolla, but the horse fund staffers are always there to steer them back to safer ground.

For now the horses are free, but for how long? The same thing that happened in Corolla is happening again to the north: Development is encroaching into the horses' habitat. Despite the remoteness of the area and lack of paved roads, or perhaps because of it, new-home construction is spreading like wildfire. Every new home built is a loss of habitat for the horses. It's getting harder and harder for the Horse Fund to protect the horses.

"Once these magnificent horses are gone, they can never return, they will be gone forever," said Donna Snow, co-director of the Corolla Wild Horse Fund. "I fear the end is closer than we want to imagine."

The Ring
·1998·

Four feet deep in the sandy soil of Hatteras Island, a team of archaeologists troweled through strata and painstakingly sifted through the earth. The team, led by Project Director Dr. David Phelps, director of East Carolina University's Coastal Archaeology Office, worked long hours, slowly and methodically, in the October sun at the "Croatan Site" on privately owned land near Cape Creek in Buxton. What they found would help them learn even more about the early residents of Hatteras Island, the Croatan Indians, one of the prominent tribes of the Carolina Algonkians.

The dig was off to a fascinating start. They had already uncovered a "workshop" where the Croatan Indians had been molding lead shot, making shell beads, and working copper into beads, figurines, and other forms, as well as trading in other European goods such as copper pins, cloth, and gun flints. Artifacts the archaeologists found in the workshop were datable, and they estimated that the workshop area dated from around 1650 to well into the 1700s.

Members of the crew had their hands in the earth at the very bottom of this dark layer of soil when they saw something strange, something made of metal. Brushing the soil away revealed a ring, worn to a dull-gray patina, with a crest visible upon its face. It was a signet ring with a side-view cutout of a lion standing on three legs, with one paw up as if in mid-prance, and its tail rising up in a curl. This was no Native American artifact!

The crew brought the excavated ring to Dr. Phelps, who was working on site. He knew from the dull-gray color of the ring that it was probably 10-karat gold. The tin and silver content in 10-karat gold would likely tarnish to that color.

The crew's excitement and curiosity was high. Since it was first recorded in 1956, the excavation site had been suggested as the location where the Croatan Native Americans associated with the Roanoke Colonies of the sixteenth century. All of the archaeologists knew not to jump to conclusions, but the thought couldn't help but cross their minds: Could this be the item that many historians hoped for, proof that the famous 1587 Lost Colony was linked to Hatteras Island? Might this be the connection between the Lost Colony and the Croatan Indians?

The "Lost Colony" is a moniker that refers to the second group of English colonists who tried to establish a permanent colony in the New World. The 112 men, women, and children arrived on Roanoke Island in 1587 with John White, who was their governor. The group had originally intended to settle farther north on the Chesapeake Bay but then decided to stay on Roanoke Island. The same month they arrived, they sent their governor, John White, back to England to get more supplies. White and the colonists agreed that if they were to move elsewhere before he got back, they would leave a sign of where they had gone. If they were in danger they would leave the symbol of a cross.

John White was delayed in England for three years. Upon his arrival in England, the country went to war with Spain, and Queen Elizabeth declared that all ships were to be used in the service of the war, not for colonization in the New World. When White finally returned to the Roanoke Island colony site in 1590, the colonists were gone and their settlement had been, for the most part, destroyed. The only clue White found to indicate where they might have moved was the letters CRO carved into a tree and CROATAN carved onto a fence post. There was no cross.

This led White to believe that the colonists had sought the help of the Croatan Indians, a friendly tribe that lived on Hatteras Island. The Croatans had been kind and helpful to the English colonists since the first explorations of 1584. Their chief, Manteo, had even been to England with Arthur Barlowe and Philip Amadas. But White was unable to go to Hatteras Island to look for the colonists, among whom were his daughter, Eleanor Dare, and granddaughter, Virginia Dare, the first English child born in the New World. As he sailed for Hatteras Island in search of the people he had left behind, a storm brewed up and the ship's captain made the decision to leave the New World for England before White could look for any traces of the colony and his family.

Historians have long debated about what happened to the colonists. Did they travel to Hatteras Island to get help from the Croatans? Did they go to the mainland? Did they go north to settle around the Chesapeake Bay as they'd originally planned? Were they killed by Indians? Did they die of starvation or drought?

Perhaps the ring Phelps' crew had found was proof that the Lost Colonists had fled to Hatteras Island. Phelps was extremely cautious about coming to that conclusion. For now the archaeologists could only be satisfied with what they knew for sure: a European-style ring that appeared to be from the Elizabethan era was found in a former Croatan Indian town site. That was all.

"This doesn't necessarily mean the Lost Colony was here," Phelps told a *Virginian-Pilot* reporter. But he did concede that the ring could guide scholars in new directions. Gold rings didn't show up at Indian sites every day, he said. As an Algonkian expert and archaeology professor, Phelps had been studying the Croatan Site in Buxton for years. He had tested the site in the early 1980s and come back in 1993 following Hurricane Emily. After that storm, Hatteras Island residents Barbara Midgett and Fred Willard were surveying Midgett's property near Cape Creek and discovered pieces of ancient pottery, bones, and clay pipe. Midgett contacted Phelps about her find.

Over several excavations at the site, Phelps had uncovered numerous artifacts, both Native American and European. But so far, most of the European artifacts could be dated to the seventeenth and early eighteenth centuries (between 1650 and 1730), sixty-five years or more after the Lost Colony's arrival.

Prior to the ring, the only item with any remote connection to the sixteenth-century English colonists was a lead musket ball with teeth marks in it. It had been recorded elsewhere that sixteenth-century military manuals advised soldiers to keep shot in their mouths at all times so that they would be ready to reload in a moment's notice, so it was presumed the musket ball indicated the presence of sixteenth-century Englishmen. After that find, Phelps was encouraged about the Elizabethan/Croatan connection, but cautiously so.

"The lead shot might be tied to the Lost Colony, but that has such a long range of history that we need something more diagnostic," Phelps told a newspaper reporter. "However," he added, "I do think this is the site where the colonists would have gone."

The gold signet ring Phelps's crew found in 1998 was taken to a Nags Head jeweler, who buffed off a section of the gray patina, revealing that it was indeed gold. The ring had been worn out; the shank was worn through and broken away.

Phelps shared the find with independent Elizabethan scholars Lebame Houston and Barbara Hird of Manteo, who, in turn, began to research the crest. It appeared to be an English nobleman's ring from the sixteenth century, the kind that was worn as a status symbol and also used for wax seals. Hopes were high that the gold ring could be tied to the Lost Colony, but there was much research to do before anyone could know for sure.

It was not difficult for Houston and Hird to trace the crest on the ring. In sixteenth-century England a coat of arms had to be granted by the College of Arms, and they were granted only to those families who had money, property, and credibility. Houston and Hird went to London to research the lion crest, called a lion passant, with John Brooke-Little at the College of Arms.

The ring was deemed a definite sixteenth-century item and was a sure connection between the Englishmen who explored the islands between 1584 and 1587 and the Native Americans of Hatteras Island. But the detective work proved that the ring was most likely not linked to the Lost Colony.

The trio identified the only family with that particular lion crest to be the Kendall family. Two men by the name of Kendall were actually part of the Roanoke colonization efforts, but they were on the 1585–1586 expedition, not the 1587 expedition of the Lost Colony.

"Master" Kendall, no first name given, was listed as a colonist who settled on Roanoke Island and explored the region around the Albemarle and Pamlico Sounds with Ralph Lane from July 1585 to June 1586. The other Kendall was Abraham Kendall, who was listed on Sir Francis Drake's ship when Drake came to check on the colony in June of 1586. (The two men could have possibly been the same person if Kendall had come on Lane's voyage but left on Drake's ship.) There were no Kendalls in the 1587 colony.

Phelps knew of one way the ring could have gotten to the site. When Lane's colony came in 1585, the contact between the Europeans and the Croatan Indians established in 1584 was immediately renewed. In 1586, Lane dispersed his forces to live with the Indians because his men were starving. A group of twenty Englishmen lived with the Croatan Indians for more than a month, which would have been ample time for a sentry to lose the tooth-marked musket ball or for Kendall to have lost the ring or given it away as a present.

Even without being able to link the ring to the Lost Colony, the scholars and archaeologists were thrilled with the find. "This is the one thing that has been found that is a personal item. And because it is a European artifact found in a Native-American village, it links the two cultures," Hird told *The Virginian-Pilot* after the discovery.

The mystery remains unsolved. No trace of the colony has ever surfaced to this day. The link to the Kendall family was not certain, though it was strong. Houston said she still needed to do follow-up research on the Kendall family to tie the ring to one of the Kendalls of the colonization efforts. Two years later, in 2000, another interesting artifact—a gunlock which may date to ca. 1584 pending further research—was found in deeper soil during excavations at the site, further adding to the long list of questions about the links between the colonists and the natives.

Archaeologists still have a lot of exploring to do in the area of Hatteras Island where the Croatan Native Americans lived. Maybe one day they will dig up the answers to all the questions that remain.

Saving the Light
• 1999 •

At the elbow-shaped bend of Hatteras Island, where the black-and-white striped Cape Hatteras Lighthouse rises over 200 feet above the sand, the hungry Atlantic swallowed huge gulps of beach, until a narrow strip of sand was all that kept the lighthouse from tumbling into the sea.

When the Cape Hatteras Lighthouse was built in 1870 it stood a solid 1,500 feet from the shoreline. But every year the sea crept closer to the beacon's base, and by 1920, the ocean waves lapped within 300 feet of the tower. Over the next several decades the lighthouse's caretakers, first the U.S. Coast Guard and then the National Park Service, made valiant efforts to stop the sea's encroachment. They constructed barriers, such as steel groins and dunes along the shoreline. They pumped mountains of sand from the Pamlico Sound and Cape Hatteras Point and placed enormous sandbags in front of the lighthouse. Then they built concrete groins and even installed innovative synthetic seaweed to widen the beach. In 1987, after decades of costly repairs to the groins and replenishment of the sandbags—at one time there were more than 300 sandbags around the lighthouse—the sea was only 120 feet from the lighthouse base. Man's battle to hold back the sea was failing.

But what could be done to save the famous American landmark?

When it came to the fate of the Cape Hatteras Lighthouse, the people of the Outer Banks were divided. While nobody denied that something had to be done to save the light, people had very different ideas about what should be done. National Park Service officials considered several protection options, including building more groins or an encircling seawall as well as relocating the tower from the ocean's edge. In 1988, the National Academy of Sciences advised them that relocation would be the most cost-effective method of protection, but it wasn't until 1996 that the National Park Service began to seek funding to move the Cape Hatteras Lighthouse a half-mile inland.

Others did not agree with this plan, including a group called the Save the Cape Hatteras Lighthouse Committee, which was absolutely opposed to moving the Cape Hatteras Lighthouse. They said it couldn't be done, that the risk was too great. They said that, in the process of moving, it would crack, or worse yet, fall. Some said that the brick mortar joints, which were then more than 125 years old, should not be stressed. The committee said they were advised by reputable construction experts and engineers that the move would not be successful. "Save Not Move" bumper stickers became prevalent on Hatteras Island and all around the Outer Banks. Many people were opposed to moving the lighthouse, not only because of the risk to the structure but also because they felt the lighthouse would lose its historical value if it was moved from its original site. "To turn tail and run by moving the lighthouse would tarnish its value as a monument to heroism," wrote Hugh Morton in the Raleigh *News and Observer* in 1998.

Cost was another factor. "It is simply not prudent to spend $12 million to obtain a zebra-striped white elephant that would not be nearly as valuable to our state if it were moved," wrote Morton.

The Dare County Commissioners and the Outer Banks Chamber of Commerce passed resolutions stating their support of keeping the lighthouse in its current location and pursuing other protection options, such as building a fourth groin and/or erosion stabilizers. But environmentalists were highly opposed to that option, and, besides, the North Carolina Division of Coastal Management would not allow it.

Debates raged, and not just on the Outer Banks. People throughout the state had an opinion on the moving of the lighthouse. The Park Service repeatedly defended its position and plans in public forums, but things got ugly. The Dare County Board of Commissioners and a group of private citizens tried to halt the move by filing a complaint and motion for a temporary restraining order, preliminary injunction, and permanent injunction in Federal court. The judge threw the case out.

"Some people have said we were apathetic about the move. The islanders were like that 'mouse that roared'—it was a done deal and a day late before we ever made our feelings known about the move," said native Buxton resident Barbara Barnett Williams in an article in *The Island Breeze*.

The National Park Service pressed ahead with its decision to move the lighthouse. The complex move required months of engineering, planning, and design. They consulted twenty-two types of technical experts, including structural, geotechnical, civil, electrical, and mechanical engineers, historic and conservation architects, surveyors and environmental scientists. The Park Service had the funds—$12 million budgeted by Congress in 1998—and the backing of a new report by North Carolina State University that said, "Move it soon—by spring 1999—or see it destroyed."

The Superintendent of Cape Hatteras National Seashore, Robert Reynolds, said, "Interim protection measures such as groins, synthetic seaweed, sandbags, and even hopeful thinking over decades have provided us with much needed time to seek the funding necessary to implement relocation. The National Park Service must pursue the option that has the best potential to preserve this important symbol for future generations. The best technical information supports relocation as the option that will secure the structure for our children's children."

Still, people worried. In editorials, letters in newspapers, and public debate, the opposition felt certain that moving the lighthouse spelled doom.

In June 1998, the National Park Service awarded the Cape Hatteras Lighthouse relocation contract to International Chimney Corporation, who subcontracted Expert House Movers of Maryland and Virginia to complete the move. The two companies had already teamed up to move three other lighthouses, and they were confident in their abilities.

The plan was to move the Cape Hatteras Lighthouse 2,900 feet south-southwest of its current location, which would place it 1,600 feet from the ocean shore, protecting it for at least another century. The lighthouse would be jacked up and slowly pushed along steel beam tracks to its new location. Along with moving the lighthouse, the Park Service planned to move all the buildings that surrounded the lighthouse, including both of the keepers' dwellings and their cisterns, the oil house, and the granite footings that once supported fencing around the tower. There would be four phases to the project: preparing the buildings and the lighthouse for the move, lifting the structures from the foundations, moving them, and stabilizing them at the new site.

Work began in December 1998, and the Cape Hatteras light beacon was extinguished in February of 1999 in preparation for the move. The lighthouse was jacked up so that workers could tunnel beneath the tower to remove its granite foundation. Expert House Movers then installed steel beams underneath the lighthouse and lifted it slowly with hydraulic jacks. On June 9, 1999, the lighthouse was 7 feet off the ground and ready for the move.

From then on, it seemed the world was watching: the park service, the local residents, Outer Banks visitors, and especially the national and international media. Satellite trucks and more than 200 media representatives rolled into Buxton in mid June.

"Failure to successfully move the lighthouse simply wasn't an option, not when you do something with as much scrutiny," said Randy Knott, one of the project engineers.

Ten thousand onlookers and the media stood in light rain on June 17 at 3:05 P.M. as the lighthouse had its first push. It moved 5 inches, which was barely perceptible to the crowd. Workers made some necessary structural checks and then went another 10 feet that day. On the second day the lighthouse was moved 72 feet. Workers played leap frog with the steel travel beams, removing the beams from behind the lighthouse and laying them in advance of the lighthouse after each push. This went on for twenty-three days. Some days there were as many as 20,000 people on site watching the monumental move. On July 9, the lighthouse moved the last 76 feet.

A month after the move, Hurricane Dennis brought a scare to the lighthouse teams. With the foundation not yet complete, Dennis pounded the Outer Banks with flooding rains and winds of 128 mph. The lighthouse stayed rooted, though some of its windows blew out and it was accessible only by raft for several days.

It took three months to finish the new foundation. In its new location the lighthouse was "straight as an arrow," reported the Park Service. Structural monitoring revealed no measurable movement or tilt. On November 12, 1999, the light was lit once again. At the relighting ceremony, all the opposition seemed to have tempered. People who had been opposed to the move were glad to see it safe. Visitors began climbing the lighthouse again in May 2000.

The move of the Cape Hatteras Lighthouse was often referred to as "the move of the century." The American Society of Civil Engineers presented the National Park Service and its team with the Outstanding Civil Engineering Achievement Award in 2000 and designated the lighthouse as a National Civil Engineering Historic Landmark. Nearly every business involved with the project received some sort of award or recognition that year.

More importantly, the historic structure was saved for future generations. Its beacon still welcomes visitors to the Outer Banks.

Isabel's Fury
· 2003 ·

In seventeen years of living on the island, John Hardison had never seen ocean water in his yard—until today. His Hatteras Village home was on the sound side of the island, 300 yards from the ocean. He began to question the decision to ignore the county's mandatory evacuation and stay at home during a hurricane. But now that the storm had arrived, it was too late to do anything else.

He was reassured by the fact that Hurricane Isabel had been downgraded to a Category 2 storm. He and his wife Judy had stuck out many such storms on the island. Days ago, when the storm had been a Category 5, the highest level hurricane possible, there had been no question that they would leave. But Isabel's wind speeds weakened considerably as the storm approached the East Coast, and their decision to stay seemed to be the right one, even though Isabel was headed straight toward the Outer Banks.

As the storm approached on the morning of September 18, 2003, John and Judy felt safe in their home on the north end of the village, where they watched The Weather Channel and listened to NOAA weather broadcasts on the radio. Judy worked on a needlepoint project, while their chocolate Labrador retriever, Maggie May, slept at her feet. It just happened to be Maggie May's birthday. The Hardisons made periodic trips out onto the deck, into the rising wind, to check the progress of the storm and to take pictures. It was on one of those trips onto the deck that John looked down and noticed the water in the yard, coming from the direction of the ocean. But it was only about a foot of water, and their house was perched atop 8-foot-tall pilings.

Fifteen minutes later, John and Judy stepped out onto the deck again. Now the water was about four feet deep, reaching halfway up the house pilings. They went back inside and decided not to go out again. The wind was becoming violent, probably getting closer to the seventy to ninety miles per hour The Weather Channel was predicting. Judy poured a glass of orange juice and settled in with her needlepoint. Meanwhile, John noticed as he looked out the window that the water was still rising. Just then, the power went out.

Around 12:30 P.M., Judy walked down the hall to the bedroom to get something for her needlepoint project. As she walked the length of the house, she noticed that the hallway floor was sloping toward the back of the house. John heard sheer terror in her voice as she screamed for him, and then he heard the worst sounds imaginable: wood splitting and cracking, and glass breaking.

"It's coming down around us!" yelled John, meaning the house. "We don't want to be in it when it goes!"

John and Judy scrambled to put on their shoes, and John grabbed a bag that contained their important papers and medications, which they had assembled earlier. They hurried to the back deck door and tried to push it open but it was jammed shut due to the shifting of the house. The house moved around them, popping and cracking in the wind. With more pressure, John was able to force the door open, but as they stepped onto the back deck, with Maggie May at their heels, they were even more disheartened. Ocean water washed around their feet, though they were standing on a deck 8 feet above the ground. All around their house the ocean rushed by, swirling massive chunks of debris toward the sound.

A loud cracking of wood sliced through the noise of the wind, and John and Judy were shocked to see their front deck washing away in the floodwaters. They had no idea what to do. The wind was extreme, their house was ripping apart, and the ocean had reached the sound. Below them was 8 or 9 feet of rushing water. There was no way out.

John noticed that an oak tree had become wedged between the house and the handrail of the stairs. Only the tiny branches of the tree top were protruding above the water, but it was their only hope. He told Judy to grab on to a limb in the tree, preferably one with leaves, which would be stronger because it was still alive. Just as he grabbed a limb of the tree himself, the back deck, where they had been standing just seconds before, broke free from the house and washed away in the swift current. John and Judy watched in horror as three-year-old Maggie May floated away in the water.

The raging flood sucked John under, but Judy was able to grab his arm and pull him up. Both of them were completely underwater except for their heads, clinging to the small limbs of the oak treetop. The water was rushing by so fast it ripped their shoes off and took John's pants. The ocean water funneled right through the Hardisons' yard, carrying decks, windows, boards, trash, and belongings from other destroyed buildings with it.

After about an hour, John's strength faltered. A man in his sixties with a variety of heart and health problems, he began to doubt his ability to hold on. "Damn it, you hold on, John! You hold on!" encouraged Judy. The couple, who'd been married for thirty years, said the Lord's Prayer and made promises to each other in the event that one of them should live and the not the other. Their faces were covered in tree bark, sand, and shredded leaves and the wind still whipped at over 90 miles an hour, but the Hardisons managed to hold on to the tree for three hours. In their company was a small tree snake, curled around a limb in the top of the oak, hanging on for life as tightly as John and Judy.

Finally, John saw a sign of hope. Keeping an eye on a neighboring house, he noticed the flood waters were slowly dropping. Soon the water had receded so that they were only waist deep in water, though they still had to cling to the tree or risk being swept away.

As the waters lowered, John and Judy witnessed a miraculous sight. Maggie May was swimming as hard as she could, going against the current to get back to her owners. She made it to the tree and hung her front paws on a piece of plywood that was wedged in the tree below John and Judy. The dog hung there for as long as she could, but was then washed away again. This time, though, she swam to a sandbar where she could stand. John and Judy followed her and felt their feet hit the ground for the first time in three and a half hours. The three of them walked through the water, back to what was left of the house. It was washed off most of its pilings, which had been snapped like matchsticks, and had moved 20 feet. It was now suspended over a 16-foot deep hole cut in the earth by the raging ocean water. Water had washed through the house, opening both ends so that you could see daylight from one end to the other.

John, Judy, and Maggie May crawled back into the house, which sat on an angled, sloped position so that the bed in the back bedroom was completely dry. The three of them huddled on the bed, in shock.

Later that day, the Hardisons heard the voices of neighbors, who were paddling by in a canoe and surveying the damage. They used the neighbor's cell phone to call their daughter, then spent one last night huddled on the dry bed in their home. The next day the sheriff and the Emergency Medical Technicians took them all to the Hatteras emergency shelter.

The north end of Hatteras Village was devastated by Hurricane Isabel, as were other parts of the Outer Banks. Though the storm was only a Category 2, it pushed a wall of water, called a storm surge, that was 6 to 8 feet above normal. The eye of the storm passed over Core Banks to the south, putting the northeast quadrant, always the worst part of a hurricane, directly over Hatteras Village for hours.

Oceanfront hotels were destroyed. The 1878 Durant Lifesaving Station, which had been converted into a hotel where Judy worked, was completely gone. Houses floated in the sound. Businesses were gutted. The oceanfront dunes were flat, and sand had swept across the entire island, which now resembled a desert. A 1,700-foot-wide breach, or inlet from the sea to the sound, opened on the north end of Hatteras Village, cutting the village off into its own island. The only way to or from the village now was by boat.

The people of Hatteras Village rallied. A friend offered John and Judy their vacation home to stay in until Easter. They had no personal belongings left, and their most treasured object became a page from one of their old photo albums that someone had found on the sound shore. Their neighbors, and even strangers, reached out to help them get back on their feet.

"People's kindness and generosity is amazing," said John. "That's one of the good things to come out of this. If not for this storm, I would've gone through life never knowing that existed in people. It has made us better people for it."

The inlet was filled and the road to Hatteras Village was rebuilt within two months. Homes and businesses were repaired, and slowly the village became fully operational again. John and Judy Hardison moved north on Hatteras Island to higher ground, but they would not be scared off the Outer Banks. In the hurricane season of 2004, they were there with the rest of the Outer Bankers, riding out the storms.

A Beach Burial

• 2005 •

As the sun came up over the water on January 15, a lone walker began her daily trek along solemn Coquina Beach, expecting the normal January sights: a vast expanse of blowing sand, a scattering of seashells and flotsam and possibly, but most likely not, another intrepid beachcomber. But on this frigid January morning, with the wind whipping from the northeast at 35 miles per hour, everything was different. Coquina Beach was a deathbed. As far as she could see, the massive bodies of black whales lay stranded on the beach, surrounded by piles of quivering sea foam. Some of the animals were still visibly breathing, but others were obviously dead, their eyes glazed and their slack jaws revealing enormous teeth.

The report of the tragedy was sent to marine biologists with the National Oceanic and Atmospheric Administration Fisheries Service and the Southeast Marine Mammal Stranding Network by 8:00 A.M. A response team organized immediately, and marine biologists and trained volunteers from all over the East Coast raced to the Outer Banks, preparing to face long days on the beach in the cold weather and wind that assaulted the islands. By late afternoon more than forty university and government scientists, biologists, and volunteers were assembled on the beach, along with a crowd of curious onlookers. With the heaviness of death hanging in the air, people wandered from whale to whale, marveling at the chance to see and put their hands on such incredible sea creatures.

After a preliminary survey of the scene, the rescuers counted thirty-one stranded short-fin pilot whales spread over a five-mile stretch of beach, just north of Oregon Inlet. The majority of the whales were female, and six of them were pregnant.

Pilot whales may be small as whales go, but weighing in at around two tons they looked enormous on the otherwise deserted stretch of beach. The morning that the whales were discovered, eighteen of them had been alive, but by the afternoon only eleven were breathing, and even those were declining fast, their hearts and lungs failing. The scientists knew that even though whales breathe air, they cannot survive on land. Used to being buoyed by water, their bodies are unable to support their own massive weight, and their lungs and hearts fail within hours of beaching. Furthermore, once they have beached, whales have very slim chances of living, even if they are returned to the water.

With little hope of saving the animals, the rescue crews did what they could to make the remaining live whales comfortable. They poured buckets of ocean water over their drying bodies, administered painkillers and sedatives, and, with heavy hearts, waited for them to die. The scientists decided to euthanize four, choosing to put them out of their misery.

It was a horrible scene of death, made worse by the fact that no one could explain with certainty what had happened or why these animals had died. According to the biologists it is not unusual to see an entire pod of pilot whales beached together. Pilot whales are very social creatures and tend to do things en masse. If one whale beached itself due to illness or because it came too close to shore in search of food, the entire pod would be likely to follow suit, even if it meant following the leader into water that was too shallow. The scientists thought that illness was a plausible cause of the beaching, since a few of the pilot whales on Coquina Beach appeared thin, with abcesses and urinary tract problems. Adding to the mystery was the question of why the whales had beached in North Carolina. Typically, pilot whale beachings occurred in Florida. The last time a pilot whale stranding occurred in North Carolina was in 1973, when a large pod washed up on Cape Lookout.

As the hours passed, other disturbing evidence entered the picture, causing people to question the sickness theory: Another whale had beached itself on the northern Outer Banks in Corolla. This time it was a lone minke whale. The next day brought more eerie news. Two pygmy sperm whales beached themselves near Buxton. Why were three species of whales dying on the Outer Banks at the same time?

While onlookers arrived at Coquina Beach to mourn the death of the whales, the scientists knew that they could find a silver lining on this very dark cloud. The dead whales represented an opportunity for them to learn about the lives of pilot whales. Rescue crews hurried to make the event something useful instead of simply something horrible. Four of the whales had already washed back into the ocean, but they had twenty-seven more animals available for study, which could help unravel the mysteries of whale behavior. Biologists hoisted some of the mammoth beasts onto stretchers and moved them closer to the dune line to keep them from washing away.

"Once you got past seeing all those animals on the beach, it became clear that we had a valuable opportunity. We needed to take advantage of it," Craig Harms, a North Carolina State University professor and veterinarian, told the Raleigh *News and Observer.*

Hoping to learn more about the beachings as well as about the species itself, the scientists began necropsies (animal autopsies) and for the next three days the beach became a fascinating outdoor laboratory. With sand blowing into their instruments, their eyes and ears, and into the depths of the exposed whale bellies, the scientists studied the whales. They sawed into the whale bodies one by one, recording every detail about the whales that they could. They took samples of tissue, urine, organs, and blood. They removed and studied unborn calves. They took DNA samples to help learn how the individual animals in the pods are related and how they relate socially. They used blood screens to test for viruses the animals were carrying. They took toxicology tests to learn what manmade chemicals the whales had been exposed to. It was a gruesome scene, but at the same time, an amazing scientific event.

As the scientists worked in their makeshift lab, discussion around the Banks and in the media continued to center on why the whales were on the beach in the first place. There were a number of possible explanations for the whale strandings. The most likely causes were a misguided search for food, illness, or inclement weather. But rumors started circulating that the Navy was to blame for the deaths. At the time the Navy was hoping to establish a 500-square-nautical-mile underwater sonar testing range off the North Carolina coast, and on January 14 and 15—the same day as the mass stranding—the USS Kearsarge Expeditionary Strike Group conducted anti-submarine exercises about 240 nautical miles from Oregon Inlet.

In a *Washington Post* article a week after the event, the Navy said it was unlikely there was any connection between the whale strandings and their deep-water sonar tests, because their tests occurred more than 200 miles from where the whales beached. The article explained that naval sonar testing had contributed to a mass whale stranding in the Bahamas in 2000, and since then environmental groups have had their eye on sonar testing and whale strandings.

Scientists theorize that sonar affects deep-diving whale species—like those that washed up at Oregon Inlet—probably because the strange sounds affect their hearing and cause them to surface too quickly. This results in decompression sickness and disorientation.

At this writing there was no conclusive evidence of how the whales died, but it was hoped that the research conducted would yield insights into the lives and deaths of these whales.

After the necropsies and tests had been completed, the scientists faced the baffling problem of what to do with the twenty-seven decaying whale bodies that lay between Coquina Beach and Oregon Inlet. Even in thirty-degree weather, the whales were decomposing rapidly. The sheer number of animals presented a problem, because the tactics employed in the past for whale removal, such as dragging them back into the ocean or even blowing them up with dynamite, would not work this time. Burial was determined to be the easiest way to dispose of the bodies. The National Park Service used backhoes to dig deep graves and the whales were buried beneath the beach.

Marine mammal strandings will continue to be a common occurrence on the Outer Banks. Due to the islands' position far out in the Atlantic Ocean, these beaches catch more sick, injured, and disoriented animals than the other beaches in the state. Out of the hundreds of marine mammal (whale, dolphin and seal) strandings in the state every year, typically half of them occur on the small portion of the northern coastline in Dare and Currituck counties. If numbers prove in the future like they have in the past, the large majority of these strandings will be dolphins, along with a few whales and seals. The cycle of nature will continue on these islands in the sea.

Index

About the Author

Molly Perkins Harrison moved to the Outer Banks after college in 1994 to work as a reporter for the local newspaper, *The Coastland Times*. Her very first assignment was to interview a 100-year-old, life-long resident of Wanchese, and that assignment instantly ignited her love of Outer Banks history. Since then she has interviewed countless "old-timers" and written about the Outer Banks in magazine and newspaper articles as well as a series of historical guidebooks, *The Corolla Walking Tour, The Manteo Walking Tour,* and *The Hatteras Island Driving Tour.* Molly is also the author of *Insiders' Guide to the Outer Banks,* twenty-third edition, and an outdoor recreation guide, *Exploring Cape Hatteras and Cape Lookout National Seashores.*

A freelance writer and editor, Molly balances time spent at her computer with practicing and teaching hatha yoga and being outside as much as possible. She lives in an almost-historic restored cottage in Nags Head with her husband and son.

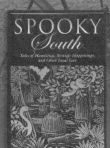

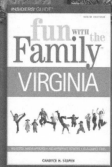
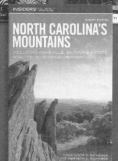